D1554483

SAINT GIUSEPPE MOSCATI

Antonio Tripodoro, S.J.

SAINT GIUSEPPE MOSCATI

Doctor of the Poor

Translated by Michael J. Miller

IGNATIUS PRESS   SAN FRANCISCO

Original Italian edition:
Giuseppe Moscati: Il medico dei poveri
Paoline Editoriale Libri
© 2004 by Figlie di San Paolo, Milan

Cover portrait by Rellie Liwag

Cover design by Riz Boncan Marsella

© 2015 by Ignatius Press, San Francisco
ISBN 978-1-58617-945-8
Library of Congress Control Number 2014959901
Printed in the United States of America ∞

CONTENTS

PREFACE

Much has been written about Giuseppe Moscati, especially after his canonization, which took place in Saint Peter's Square on October 25, 1987. His reputation as a physician dedicated particularly to the poor—or "pro-bono doctor", as he was called—attracted everyone's attention and gave rise to an indescribable wave of sympathy. The fact that he was a physician, to whose intercession countless graces of healing have been attributed, made him popular and spread devotion to him far and wide.

His tomb in the Church of the Gesù Nuovo is the constant destination of pilgrimages, and the faithful can be found there at all hours of the day, praying and kissing the hands of the bronze statue and of the sculpted figure on the tomb where his body rests. These hands have been polished to a shine by the caresses of the devotees.

Furthermore, if we are to believe a great number of testimonies, which are published now and then in the bimonthly magazine *Il Gesù Nuovo*, edited in Naples, the saint manifests his presence in dreams or in particular circumstances, announcing a healing or giving significant signs. The walls of the "Moscati Room" adjacent to the Church of the Gesù Nuovo are covered with *ex voto* offerings, tangible signs of thanksgiving for the graces received.

Nor can we fail to mention the spiritual graces obtained through the intercession of the saint—graces that are more hidden, but no less numerous or important.

In reading his biography, we are fascinated by his personality, as were those who knew him and dealt with him while he was alive. It was impossible not to admire him and to be charmed by him. His teaching, his professional credentials, his detachment from money and his interest in the poor earned him respect, sympathy and affection. Even those who were far from the faith were won over by his work and, especially after his death, gave explicit testimony to that effect.

We all feel sometimes the need to meet someone whose life can show us higher values and trustworthy goals. Giuseppe Moscati was such a person. He is the man who was able to reconcile science and faith and who, by his work, communicated to others the fruits of this synthesis. In doing so he was benevolent, understanding, charitable and not attached to worldly goods. His writings, which have an unmistakable style, are always filled with lofty sentiments of great spiritual value that tend to communicate serenity and peace.

In composing these pages I relied very much on the testimonies of those who lived alongside the saint and had a relationship with him, especially his students and colleagues. These testimonies were always given under oath as part of the canonical processes for his beatification and canonization.

I hope that acquaintance with the saintly doctor, our contemporary, may bear good fruit for the readers and prompt them to imitate him. In today's world, which is rich in technological progress but often lacking in sensitivity for the poor and the suffering, his life can be a word to the wise and an encouragement to bring about a climate of solidarity and greater understanding.

CHRONOLOGY

7/25/1880   Giuseppe Moscati is born in Benevento, a son of Francesco and Rosa de Luca.

7/31/1880   He is baptized with the names Giuseppe Maria Carlo Alfonso.

1881–1884   His father is promoted to Judge of the Court of Appeals and moves with his family to Ancona; in 1884 he is appointed Presiding Judge of the Court of Appeals in Naples.

12/8/1888   Giuseppe receives his First Holy Communion from Monsignor Enrico Marano in the Church of the Handmaids of the Sacred Heart.

1889–1897   He enrolls in the secondary school affiliated with the Vittorio Emanuele Institute. In 1897 he earns a classical diploma and enrolls in the Faculty of Medicine.

12/21/1897   His father dies.

3/2/1898   He receives the Sacrament of Confirmation, conferred on him by Bishop Pasquale de Siena, Auxiliary Bishop of Cardinal Sanfelice.

8/4/1903   Giuseppe earns a degree in medicine. In that same year he wins the competition for temporary assistant at the Ospedali Riuniti.

6/2/1904   His brother Alberto dies.

1908	Regular Assistant Professor at the Institute of Physiological Chemistry.
1911	Helps victims of cholera. Temporary Assistant at the Ospedali Riuniti. Associate member of the Royal Academy of Medicine and Surgery.
1911–1923	Teaching at the Ospedale degli Incurabili (Hospital for Incurables).
11/25/1914	His mother dies.
1919	Head Physician of the Third Men's Ward of the Ospedale degli Incurabili.
10/14/1922	University Teaching Qualification for courses in general clinical medicine.
4/12/1927	Dies in his house on the via Cisterna dell'Olio.
11/16/1930	Translation of his body to the Church of the Gesù Nuovo in Naples.
7/6/1931	Beginning of the diocesan process of documenting his reputation for sanctity.
5/10/1973	Decree issued on his heroic virtues by the Congregation for the Causes of Saints.
11/16/1975	Beatification in Saint Peter's Square.
11/16/1977	Translation of his body to the altar of the Visitation, in the Church of the Gesù Nuovo.
4/28/1987	Approval of the miraculous healing of Giuseppe Montefusco of acute non-lymphoid leukemia.
10/25/1987	Canonization in Saint Peter's Square.

From the Sabato to Vesuvius

Santa Lucia di Serino is a town of very ancient origin in the Italian province of Avellino. In its territory are found tombs from the third and fourth century B.C. and also remains of the Claudius Aqueduct, which supplied the Roman military port of Miseno. It is situated on the right bank of the Sabato River, which flows also through Benevento.

In Santa Lucia di Serino the Moscati family boasts of well-documented origins going back to the sixteenth century.

There, on October 12, 1836, was born Francesco Moscati, Giuseppe's father, who took a degree in law at the University of Naples and had a brilliant career on the judicial bench. He served as a judge in the Court of Cassino, presiding judge of the Court of Benevento, judge of the Court of Appeals in Ancona and, lastly, presiding judge of the Court of Appeals in Naples. In Cassino he married Rosa de Luca, who was descended from the Marquis of Roseto. Their marriage was blessed by the Abbot of Monte Cassino, Father Luigi Tosti, a famous historian who is remembered in the events of the Italian *Risorgimento*: in 1849 he had exhorted Pius IX to renounce his temporal power as ruler of the Papal States.

The Moscatis had nine children: Giuseppe was the seventh.

The first five children were born in Monte Cassino: Gennaro, Alberto, the twins Maria and Anna, who died of diphtheria in 1875, and another Maria; in Benevento—Anna, who died four years after Giuseppe did; in Ancona—Eugenio and Domenico.

The Moscatis had moved to Benevento in 1877, when Francesco was promoted to presiding judge of the court, and they took up lodgings on the via San Diodato, in the vicinity of the hospital. After a few months they changed their residence and settled in an apartment on the via Port'Aurea, near the Arch of Trajan, in the Andreotti Palace, which was later acquired by the Leo family, the present owners. There, on July 25 in the year 1880, Giuseppe came into the world.

In those days, Benevento had been annexed to the Kingdom of Italy for two decades, but obviously this change of course had not nullified the previous centuries of papal rule. As in other cities, here too the religious were expelled, the lands and goods of the convents were seized, archives were confiscated and the buildings that had belonged to the clergy were occupied, with resulting damage that can be imagined. Freemasonry had a free hand, and the wind of anticlericalism was blowing unabated.

To Benevento the Moscatis brought their faith and a constant fidelity to Christian principles, and they took the trouble to give their children a religious education. The parents were fervent Christians, as we know from their son Eugenio who, in the diocesan process in Naples concerning the virtues of the then Servant of God Giuseppe Moscati, testified as follows:

Our parents ... were very fervent practicing Christians, and proof of this is their scrupulosity in educating us in the bosom of the Catholic religion by their regular attendance to their Christian duties and by the daily recitation in common of the Holy Rosary of our Lady.... We were all educated at home. According to the custom of our household, the Servant of God was baptized immediately and to him was given the name of Giuseppe, followed by Maria, as our parents did with all their male children, and then other names that I do not remember. He received the Sacrament of Confirmation at the age of twelve or thirteen, if I recall correctly. His sponsor was Signor Cosenza of Naples. What I have testified I learned firsthand. (PSV, §4)

Presiding Judge Francesco, as a boy, had thought about religious life but had been dissuaded from it by the Redemptorist Father Ribera, who had presented to him the Christian ideal that he could put into practice while exercising the profession of judge.

As for his mamma, Signora Rosa, who went to heaven on November 25, 1914, when her son Giuseppe had already earned distinction as a professor, let us recall what she said to her children on her deathbed, after receiving the sacraments: "My dear children, you cause me to die happy: always flee from sin, which is the greatest evil in life."

In the Moscati family, religiosity was a tradition and an inheritance. Among the family members of earlier generations there was even a Jesuit Father, Domenico Antonio Moscati, who in the seventeenth century was a man of letters and a philosopher, who by his writings spread devotion to Mary Immaculate.

The education imparted to the children was in keeping with the social rank of the family, with the position
held by the presiding judge of the Court of Appeals in
Naples and also with their economic status, since the Moscati and De Luca families were comfortably well off. The
boys had their own tutor, who supervised their studies and
cultural formation.

Every year Judge Moscati spent his vacation with his
family in their native region, in Santa Lucia di Serino, and
he dedicated many hours of the day to the children, having
them take long walks through the fields and the nearby
mountains, where there were plenty of trees, lakes and ani-
mals. Every day he attended Mass in the chapel of his ances-
tral palace or in the seventeenth-century church of Santa
Maria della Sanità at the monastery of the Poor Clares,
setting an example for his children, because he always received Communion and, when he could, served at the altar.

"His Honor the Presiding Judge," wrote Sister Maria
Chiarina Rossi to Nina Moscati on January 28, 1928,
"sometimes served Mass and very much enjoyed carrying the canopy over the Blessed Sacrament when It was
exposed during the month of October. He and the boys
all used to remain kneeling for a long time like statues."[1]

Religiosity and education went hand in hand for the
high-ranking magistrate.

One year after Peppino's [Giuseppi's] birth, the Moscati
family moved to Ancona, in the Marches, which in the past
had been part of the Papal States, although Freemasonry
prevailed there now. Public officials, in order to keep their

[1] A. Marranzini, *La chiesa di Santa Maria della Sanità: Monastero delle Clarisse in
Santa Lucia di Serino* (Salerno: Elea Press, 1993), 52.

post and advance in their career, were often compelled to join the sect and to stop performing their religious duties. Presiding Judge Francesco, however, held firm and never submitted to the moral extortion coming from various parties. He remained true to his principles and as always, together with his family, attended Mass and received Communion. Usually he went to the church of Saints Cosmas and Damian, in the vicinity of the piazza della Posta, the site of the Palazzo Rosini, his place of residence.

For him faith in God was greater than external pressures and the fear that merely human considerations could strike in him.

In those days Peppino was too little to understand the difficulties and the courageous resistance of his father, but he inherited that courage, and later on, whenever he noticed injustices and abuses of power, he energetically rebelled and, like his father, never compromised his own conscience. The constant uprightness of the parents' conduct could not help shaping beneficially the future life of their children!

Three years later, Francesco Moscati was promoted to the Court of Appeals in Naples, with assignments to the sessions of the Court of Assizes in Santa Maria Capua Vetere. This transfer was greeted with joy by the whole family. There would be no more antireligious pressures, and the children, in a rural setting, would be able to have an education more in keeping with their family traditions.

When they came to Naples, the Moscati family took up lodgings at 83 via Santa Teresa al Museo; next in the Bagnara Palace on the piazza Dante, in apartment 89; for several months on the via Sant'Anna dei Lombardi and, finally, at 10 via Cisterna dell'Olio.

The gulf, the peninsula of Sorrento and Mount Vesuvius, whose plume of smoke rose into the sky, surely must have piqued the curiosity of little four-year-old Peppino and many times cause him to marvel at it. Later on, as a young physician, when Vesuvius displayed its destructive power, Doctor Moscati was among the first to come to the aid of the poor patients.

2

A Model Student

In Naples, the Moscati family began to enjoy the serenity for which they had long hoped and finally gained.
Signora Rosa de Luca of the Marquis of Roseto and the
Presiding Judge of the Court of Appeals of Naples, Francesco, diligently performed their duties as parents: they
had a certain dignity about them, a lofty social rank, an
enviable reputation, but above all a profound faith. They
knew very well the importance of a sound education
and were certainly convinced of the influence of their
example on the minds of their children. The mother, at
home, personally took care of the education of the boys,
while the father went out with them and lovingly guided
them, often accompanying them to church to visit the
Blessed Sacrament.

On December 8, 1888, little Giuseppe had his first
encounter with the eucharistic Jesus, after being prepared
by Monsignor Enrico Marano, who celebrated the Mass
in the church of the Handmaids of the Sacred Heart. No
other details of the event have come down to us, but we
can say that on that day was laid the foundation of his
eucharistic life, which was one of Professor Moscati's
secrets of sanctity.

After his elementary studies, Giuseppe enrolled in secondary school and, from the academic year 1889–1890 on, attended the Vittorio Emanuele Institute.

The effect on him of state school was at first traumatic, but talent and good will soon triumphed: he was promoted each year, and even became the first of his class. In 1897, when he earned his secondary school diploma, he came out first among the ninety-four students enrolled. His academic record, which can still be seen in the school archives, is impressive: an eight in written Italian and in translation from Latin and a nine in translation from Greek; in his oral examinations: ten in Italian, Latin, Greek and history; nine in philosophy, physics, chemistry and natural history; eight in mathematics. Among the professors' signatures are those of the Latinist Giuseppe Petrone and the priest Giuseppe Mercalli, the famous volcanologist and seismologist, inventor of the "intensity scale" that is named after him. Professor Petrone, as a classmate of Moscati reported, often used to say to students in other classes: "Let us seek to imitate my scholar Moscati. He is the pearl of the youth, not only because of his studiousness, but also because of his behavior and seriousness."

In this connection his brother Eugenio testified:

From the first year of the *gymnasium* [middle school] to the third year of the *lyceum* [preparatory school] he studied at the Regio Liceo Vittorio Emanuele in Naples. He was always the first in his class in all eight years. His teachers loved him and held him in high esteem above every other student, and I, who had almost all the same teachers at the Liceo as he did, heard him being held up as an example, frequently, even and perhaps especially by the professors who had the reputation of being very strict, such as Professor Giuseppe Petrone. One of his teachers is still alive, Professor Giuseppe Caroselli. (PSV, §§4–5)

During this period of studies, while Giuseppe was attending fourth-year classes in middle school—this was in 1892—his brother Alberto, who eight years earlier had entered the Military Academy in Turin, fell from a horse during a military parade and suffered cranial trauma resulting in epilepsy with Jacksonian seizures. In 1894 Alberto returned to his parents' house in Naples, and only then did the whole family realize the seriousness of the illness. Sometimes the convulsions lasted as long as twenty-four hours.

This accident of the second-born son was traumatic for them all, and Giuseppe, ten years younger, spent long hours beside his brother: in his close relative he experienced the tragedy of suffering and observed the need to alleviate it, at least by one's affectionate presence. Did he think in those days about his future career? We do not know, but it is certain that some important decisions in life are not unforeseen.

Alberto went away in 1902 to live with the Brothers Hospitallers of St. John of God in Benevento, but the illness never left him, until he died on June 2, 1904, with a rosary in his hands and the crucifix on his chest.

Having brilliantly passed his final examinations in classics, Giuseppe, who was then eighteen years old, found that he needed to choose on what career he should embark. As is the case for all young men, this was an important decision that would set the direction for his future.

One would think that his father, a renowned judge, knowing his son's intelligence and poise, might want him to go into law and then become a judge, but he soon realized that that was not going to happen. Convinced that his sons had to feel free in choosing their own professions, he offered no resistance when Giuseppe assured him that he would enroll in the faculty of medicine. His mother, who knew her son's sensibility well and anticipated his excessive dedication to the duties that he would be assuming, expressed hesitation about his decision and tried to dissuade him, but his response was firm: "But what are you saying, Mamma? I am ready even to lie down in the patient's bed."

At a distance of about a century, today we too wonder how young Giuseppe ever chose the medical profession, contrary to the expectations of his family, which boasted of traditions in the field of law (besides his father, his brother Gennaro too had embarked on this career and after him so would his brother Domenico). Fortunately we have several answers in this connection, and they all converge on just one motive. Let all of them be represented by what was written by Professor Gaetano Quagliariello, who was then Rector of the University of Naples and a very dear friend of Moscati.

> Not a preference for the study of medicine, about which he, having grown up in a family of jurists, had no particular knowledge, nor the ambition to win someday the aura of popularity and celebrity that everywhere and in every age has surrounded and still surrounds physicians who succeed in asserting their personality, much less the desire to create for himself a brilliant position in society, but only the desire, which in his

good soul had already become an imperious necessity, to alleviate the physical pain, the spiritual bewilderment of brethren who are struck by the atrocity of diseases, made him choose the medical profession. (GQ, pp. 87–88)

Having commenced his studies in medicine, the first seriously ill patient whom Giuseppe confronted was, of all people, his father. He had been attending the University for scarcely two months and, as always, his family was preparing to celebrate Christmas. On December 19, 1897, Judge Moscati walked across the piazza Dante, turned to the right and went to the Archconfraternity of the Santissima Trinità dei Pellegrini of which he was a member, to attend Sunday Mass. Shortly afterward he felt ill and, returning the same way that he had walked shortly before, he went back to his house on the via Santa Teresa al Museo. At around eleven o'clock he had a cerebral hemorrhage; the doctors did everything they could to save him but managed to keep him alive only two days. On December 21, 1897, he asked to receive the sacraments and spoke with his first-born son Gennaro, to whom he entrusted his mother and his siblings; moreover he recommended that his remains be brought to the cemetery in Serino, alongside those of his dear relatives. At eleven-thirty he gave up his spirit to God.

Giuseppe was shaken by this unexpected death for several reasons: it was the first time that he was in the presence of a departed loved one; with his father he lost his most valuable counselor and the one who could have guided him now that he had embarked on his university studies; his sick brother Alberto would be a heavy burden for the family; from that day on their financial situation would not be as carefree as before: his mother and his older brother, besides Alberto, would have to look after him, his sister Anna and his brothers Eugenio and Domenico, who were fifteen and thirteen years old respectively.

His father's death left a gaping hole in the young man's life, and he would always remember it with sorrow, but also with profound resignation. In 1925, twenty-eight years later, while writing to his assistant, Doctor Michele Guglielmi, who had just lost his father, he would say: "I understand the anguish of your family! I too experienced it, as a boy: my father was an upright judge, like your dear departed father; and it seemed that he had left his family abandoned! But God replaces the one whom He wants to have by His side. And you and yours will feel the mysterious, invisible protection that your parent's soul will lavish upon you!" (AM, p. 287).

The oldest brother, the lawyer Gennaro, took charge of the family after the father's death and continued to head it earnestly and worthily. He was twenty-eight years old and proved to be up to the task that his father had entrusted to him before he died: to take his place with regard to the younger siblings.

His brother Eugenio later recalled that Giuseppe, "although he had reached a mature age and had attained scientific renown, when in our family, for whatever reason, any disagreement arose, especially between him and my oldest brother, the late Gennaro Moscati, Esquire— who was like a father to us and had a rather strong, severe personality—a disagreement in which I saw, quite simply, that my brother Giuseppe was right, he on the contrary would remain silent and would comply with the decision and the statements of our older brother" (PSV, §69).

3

University Studies

The Young Doctor Braves the Eruption of Vesuvius
in 1906 and the Cholera Epidemic of 1911

When Giuseppe Moscati enrolled in the faculty of medicine
at the University of Naples, the number of students aver-
aged around one thousand five hundred, while there were
thirty-four professorial chairs. Among the very important
ones were the professorships in anatomy, physiology, general pathology, clinical surgery and so forth. The curric-
ulum of studies provided for twenty-three courses with
examinations in each, arranged in three two-year periods.
Among the first professors whom Giuseppe encountered
in the first biennium were Pietro Castellino, Giuseppe
Albini, Giovanni Paladino and Nicola Pane.

The atmosphere that everyone breathed at the University was certainly not optimal from the ethical and
religious viewpoint, since there was blowing a political
sectarian, Masonic wind that originated from two cen-
ters: the faculty of philosophy and the faculty of medicine. Fichtean and Hegelian idealism ruled in the former,
together with the liberal, secularist theories of Bertrando
Spaventa; in the latter, materialistic positivism attributed

an absolute, quasi-divine status to matter, rejecting any metaphysical or transcendent reality.

The young men were easy prey for the prophets of agnosticism and atheism, also because they were carried away by the revolutionary, sectarian wave that was dominant then.

Giuseppe kept his distance from all extremism and, understanding that his main occupation was to study, he avoided everything that might distract him. Moreover he knew very well that serious, deep study requires tranquility and serenity of spirit. How could he have applied himself to his work if he had followed so many of his companions who were creating disturbances and shouting in the public squares?

"He sat beside me and was attentive, serious, rather composed," testified Professor Bevacqua, his classmate at clinic of the Ospedale degli Incurabili, "but what really impressed me was the way in which he, although just a beginner, answered all the questions that the professor asked the students, to himself, without being heard by anyone, except by those who were very near; there was no question, even a difficult one, that he did not answer promptly, even though it went without an answer from the more experienced students."[1]

This reminiscence of a classmate who sat in the lecture hall with Giuseppe is particularly interesting, because it gives a glimpse not only of his natural talents but also of a deliberate attitude, almost a stance that he took toward a task that he considered his primary duty. This habit of

---

[1] C. Testore, *Il professor Giuseppe Moscati della Regia Università di Napoli* (Naples: F. Giannini, 1934), 20–21.

answering all the questions, even difficult ones, when the more experienced students could not do so, was the expression of a constant, conscious, intelligent commitment. From the beginning he had understood that it was not enough to earn a degree in medicine, but that he had to prepare well in order to approach the infirmities of his neighbor. And in his neighbor he saw God himself.

As his studies became more complex and difficult, he felt more urgently the need to reconcile science and charity, blending them into a vital synthesis. This synthesis would always flourish when, having become an established doctor who was in demand, he would visit the sick and write prescriptions. In the sick person he would see a body and a soul, both in need of help. For him, being a physician did not mean being just any professional; rather, it meant that he had chosen and accepted a *sublime mission*.

"Remember", he wrote on September 4, 1921, to his student of three years Doctor Giuseppe Biondi, when he earned his degree in medicine, "that in pursuing medicine you have assumed responsibility for a sublime mission. Persevere, with God in your heart, with the teachings of your father and your mother always in your memory, with love and devotion for the abandoned, with faith and enthusiasm, deaf to praises and criticisms, steadfast against envy and inclined only to do good" (AM, p. 232).

At the age of eighteen he received the Sacrament of Confirmation, conferred on him on March 2, 1898, by Bishop Pasquale de Siena, an Auxiliary Bishop of Cardinal Sanfelice. His sponsor was Francesco Saverio Cosenza, a friend of the family. From the full outpouring of the Holy Spirit he received the strength to live out his faith intensely and to witness to it in all circumstances.

In the university setting he continued to distinguish himself by his seriousness and diligence, by which he soon attracted the attention not only of his classmates but also of the professors. In July of 1898 he applied himself so studiously that he won first prize for the best examination in zoology, whereas every year—as his brother Eugenio assures us—"he received a dispensation from the examination fees and got the maximum number of votes in all subjects."

On August 4, 1903, he received his medical degree. Giuseppe defended a thesis on hepatic urogenesis, and at the conclusion he received the maximum number of votes, praise, the applause of the board of examiners and a special recommendation whereby the work was declared worthy of publication. That is all that we know. It is unknown whether it actually was published, nor do we have evidence or testimonies to that effect, because the archives of the University of Naples were destroyed during the Second World War.

On the same day as the thesis defense, in Rome, Cardinal Giuseppe Sarto was elected Pope, taking the name Pius X. Among the mementos of Moscati that are preserved in the Moscati Room at the Church of Gesù Nuovo, there is a picture of Pius X with this inscription: "To Giuseppe Moscati, on whom was conferred a degree in medicine and surgery on the same day on which Pius X was crowned with the papal tiara, Filomena dei Marchesi de Filippi, admirer of the scientific knowledge and the virtue of the young laureate, dedicates and presents on July 4, 1904, this image of the Supreme Pontiff, a reminder of so great a coincidence."

The admirer of the scientific knowledge and the virtue of the young degree recipient was a descendent of a family from Santa Lucia di Serino, whose palace is situated a short distance from that of the Moscatis. Therefore she knew Giuseppe well and could guess that he would be a man of science and a model of virtue.

In 1902, one year before Giuseppe's doctorate, the Moscati family moved to the third floor of a spacious building on the via Cisterna dell'Olio, at number ten. To get to it, one enters by a rather large front gate that admits the visitor to a small courtyard, from which a steep, narrow stairway leads to the upper floors. The palazzo is located exactly midway between the piazza Dante and the piazza del Gesù Nuovo, where the church of Gesù Nuovo of the Jesuit Fathers faces the church of Santa Chiara of the Franciscan Fathers. From then on these would be the favorite churches of Giuseppe, who would pass in front of them every day to go to the University and to the Ospedale degli Incurabili.

After receiving his degree, the young doctor had one success after another, and while he distinguished himself by his intelligence and knowledge, his love for his neighbor grew within him. Two events in particular illustrate his selfless charity.

On April 8, 1906, Vesuvius, which had always been an object of curiosity, admiration and inspiration for many artists, reawakened and, as on other occasions in history, began to manifest its tremendous destructive force. From its crater issued horrific streams of lava, stones and ash, which poured down the slopes of the mountain, threatening the neighboring towns and terrorizing the inhabitants.

The writer Matilde Serao, in a realistic, ghastly description of those days that appeared in the daily newspaper *Il Mattino* on April 22, 1906, revealed on the one hand the devastating fury of the mountain, and on the other hand the flight of the weary, destitute, disheartened people.

> Whilst on every side, from every person, from every telephonic communication, from every telegram, the most distressing news reach us, whilst the first impulse is to set out, to run there, where people are suffering, where they are agonizing with fright and sorrow, we all know that the Circumvesuviana railway is interrupted, and we understand how difficult it is to go there quickly, or in any useful way.... We leave Naples by carriage, in the afternoon. The city has a depressed look and is unusually quiet. And gradually, as we cross from Ponte della Maddalena to San Giovanni a Teduccio, the last people on the road disappear.... All along the streets, on the sidewalks, in the shops, silence is increasing, getting more intense, more profound....
>
> Our mind is getting depressed, and our sadness increases when we see the utter silence and complete solitude of Resina and Torre del Greco, the lovely little towns situated between gardens of orange trees, and the sea. Unheard-of squalor, as in a city where all life had disappeared, where every form of life whatsoever had been scattered. The charming cities of Portici, Resina and Torre del Greco are now completely dead and deserted, not a soul is left there. They look as though they had been dead and deserted for many, many years. Nobody is there to tell us the panic, the terrible panic that has set these people flying for safety in the night, at dawn, in the morning; but we know it, we can easily imagine it since we see with our mortal eyes, abandonment and death everywhere. But did Resina, Portici and

Torre del Greco ever live? Were there ever people in these houses, in these streets? Like an immense colossus the pine-shaped cloud of ash rises on the mountain, and everything is shut out from our sight on account of the ashes, clouds and vapors filling the air. Only the lightning is visible, the hundred flashes cutting the livid and opaque gray. And life is only there on the mountain of horrors, whilst here nothing more is living.[2]

Right in Torre del Greco, a town nestled in the foothills of Vesuvius and only six kilometers [three and three-quarter miles] distant from the crater, the Ospedali Riuniti [United Hospitals] of Naples had an affiliated residence for the sick and the elderly, all of whom were unable to move about. What we are imagining now, thinking of the terror and despair of the poor residents, was certainly on the mind of young Doctor Moscati in those days, when he experienced with the Neapolitans the tragedy in his city and in the other neighboring cities. Witnessing the scenes described by Signora Serao, he would have thought of how anxious those unfortunate souls were to escape, to run far away, to save themselves. But how? Who could help them, if everyone in that region could barely manage to bring himself and his own family to safety, drawing carts loaded with furniture?

All of his biographers describe the decision and the efforts of Doctor Moscati on that occasion: he went to Torre del Greco, reached the hospital, delivered to the director the order to clear out and he himself helped the

---

[2] Matilde Serao, *Sterminator Vesevo: Vesuvius the great Exterminator: Diary of the eruption of April 1906*, translated by L. H. (Naples: Francesco Perrella, 1907), 51–52, 54–55, slightly emended.

most disabled to leave the building and take their places on the motor vehicles that were to bring them to Naples. Meanwhile the sky had darkened, the ash fell more and more thickly and was accumulating heavily on the streets, in the courtyards and on the roofs. The roof of the hospital could no longer hold under the increasing weight and after a short time collapsed. Fortunately the last resident had just left the building.

What the young doctor experienced at that moment is easy to imagine. He had performed his duty, saved several human lives, given aid to the most needy. Providence too, this time, had not forgotten the weakest and had made use of his desire to do good. But who was he? A humble servant who had only done his duty. Therefore, humbly and with conviction, two days later he sent a confidential letter to the general director of health of the Ospedali Riuniti of Naples, proposing a reward for the inspector, Signor Giovanni Astarita, who had accompanied him; a bonus for four male nurses "to whose discipline and devotion to me I owe a large part of the very good result of my expedition"; some recompense for the female nurses "who under a downpour of ashes and slag helped me to transport the patients"; and praise for the nuns and the father rector "who calmly gave much moral assistance".

And for him? Absolutely nothing: "Certain," he declares, "that anyone of my station would have done the same and better; and therefore I implore you to combine any personal praise with the praises for the president and the general director, who inspire by their example, with the praises for their colleagues, for the employees, whose selfless work in these sad days I have been admiring as a spectator, a friend and a man with a heart—work that is superior to all envy and worthy only of emulation." Then he concludes with a witticism: "I entreat you to continue along these lines, so as not to stir up ... the ashes!" (AM, pp. 95–96).

In those days Moscati was a temporary assistant at the Ospedali Riuniti, and the administration publicly commended him for having saved seventy paralyzed residents in the Ospedale di Torre del Greco.

General Martinelli, too, who had been sent to Naples to aid the populations struck by the disastrous eruption, sent a letter to the Ministry of the Interior praising Doctor Moscati's rescue work. In turn the Government acknowledged that Moscati's courage had spared the United Hospitals the dire consequences that occurred in Naples because of the collapse of the Monteoliveto market.

Unfortunately, his habit of staying in the background "so as not to stir up ashes", as he had written to the general director of health of the Ospedali Riuniti of Naples, prevents us from knowing in detail about his zealous work on the occasion of another scourge that afflicted Naples and spread fear and trepidation everywhere: cholera.

In 1911, as had happened on other occasions, a cholera epidemic began to spread among the people and with it an understandable terror. In a port city, where ships from all over the world docked, and where the alleys were not renowned for their cleanliness, hygiene and morality, and where poverty was habitual, anything could happen. Luckily though, in comparison with past incidents, medicine and treatment had made enormous advances and therefore the number of casualties was limited.

All that we know about the work performed by Moscati is that he was called by the Ministry to the Laboratory of the Board of Public Health, to the Prefecture itself, in order to conduct research into the origin of the disease and suitable methods for combating it. He accomplished this task as usual with the utmost diligence, submitted a report on the projects necessary to restore health in the city, and he had the satisfaction of seeing that many of his proposals were carried out.

In that same year, 1911, earth-shaking events occurred: Germany displayed its growing military power and caused concerns in several nations; Italy declared war against Turkey; ships loaded with soldiers departed from Naples for Libya, and they were cheered enthusiastically by those who were unaware of the fate that awaited them there. The "bard" Gabriele D'Annunzio incited Italians to conquer the "fourth border".

4

Scientific Preparation
and Victory in Competitions

After he earned a doctorate—as was noted—on August 4, 1903, the university and the hospital were the areas in which the young physician worked; he attended to his research and scientific production with extraordinary commitment. Very soon the fruits thereof were evident, since in December of 1903, the same year as his doctorate, Moscati won the competition for temporary assistant at the Ospedale degli Incurabili and in 1908 placed second out of twenty-one in the competition for regular assistant at the Institute of Chemical Physiology, which allowed him to use the laboratory and conduct scientific research. In the test for the position of temporary assistant, Moscati astounded everyone, because he even beat the contenders who were interns and were scored one-fifth higher than he, who was merely an extern.

In that same period he won a competition for a position to study at the "Aquarium" in Naples, founded by A. Dohrn, which at the time was a meeting place for researchers and great scientists from Italy and abroad. Later on he also won competitions for head of the laboratory of the Third Medical Clinic, directed by Professor Gaetano

Rummo; for assistant in the laboratory of the Ospedale Cotugno; and for medical officer in Naples, a post which he did not accept.

Considering his work in that period and the promising results, which he owed not only to his basic education during his years at the university but especially to his diligent study and scientific research, one might ask where he found the time for such careful and extensive preparation.

Professor Quagliariello tells us the answer: "working twelve hours a day, he scientifically and conscientiously performed manifold duties, but little by little his efforts centered on the Incurabili and the University. And these were eight years of tireless, silent work in which he enriched his mind with books and with his experience in the laboratory and at the bedside of the sick, allowing for his professional practice the minimum necessary to provide for the material needs of his austere and very simple way of life" (GQ, p. 90).

To conclude this list of the accomplishments of the young doctor, who was only a little more than twenty years old, we merely recall the very promising evaluation of his study of November 1906: "Starch Indicator Injected into the Organism", presented to the Medical-Surgical Academy and endorsed by Professors Pasquale Malerba, Gaetano Jappelli and Francesco Arena: "The research by Doctor Moscati, because of the seriousness with which it was conducted, the precision of the methods employed and the extensive documentation, has attracted the attention of the entire committee, which praises the author highly."

And the final remarks: "The board applauds Doctor Moscati and proposes that his study be published in its entirety in the *Atti della Reale Accademia* [Acts of the Royal Academy]. Furthermore it proposes Doctor Moscati as an adjunct associate in the eventuality of a vacancy. Naples, November 1906. The Board: P. Malerba, F. Arena, G. Jappelli secretary."

The following year, 1907, the Academy, again in the name of the Board made up of Malerba, Arena and Jappelli, bestowed more high praise on him for a second study and concluded: "The board, after having praised the author and encouraged him to continue his scientific research, proposes that the two studies be published in the Acts of the Academy, and in addition makes so bold as to repeat its proposal that the name of Moscati, who is so distinguished for his diligence, knowledge and abilities, should be kept in mind for an appointment as resident adjunct associate."

Although Moscati was scarcely twenty-seven years old, everyone admired his seriousness, his vast knowledge and a scientific rigor that presaged ever loftier accomplishments.

And he achieved one of these goals in the 1911 competition, which has remained famous in Naples in medical circles. Indeed, the award had not been conferred since 1880 and therefore the most highly educated doctors and instructors in Naples and Southern Italy took part in it. The number of contestants was quite large and there were only six posts. To win one meant being one step away from the highest responsibilities, since, as Professor Quagliariello wrote, "The head physicians of hospitals and those who are qualified to give lectures in infirmaries come exclusively from among the coadjutors. The board of examiners was made up of men like Antonio Cardarelli, Enrico De Renzi and Beniamino De Ritis" (GQ, p. 90).

Unfortunately, as often happens on similar occasions, everyone resorted to recommendations, subterfuges and interventions by influential persons. At stake was the attainment of a high-ranking position, and no one wanted to miss out on the opportunity. Thus preparation and merit were no longer to be rewarded, but rather "the cowardice of copying" and the "dishonest, dastardly plan of competition hatched by a few".

These are the words of Moscati himself, who on several occasions before the examinations had already come to know about frequent underhanded competition and various schemes devised by some to pass the written test. In particular he foresaw and feared that many would copy the work of others and present it as their own. Therefore on April 5 and then on April 20 he wrote two fiery letters, which have come down to us: one addressed to Professor Giovanni Boeri, a regular professor of medical pathology, the other to Professor Alfonso Calabrese, a regular professor of clinical medicine.

To the former he wrote, among other things:

> Since it has been reported to me that perhaps you will pose a personal question so that the competition for coadjutor at the Incurabili might proceed without tampering and without the dishonesty of copying and cheat sheets, I, rather than be complacent, must inform you that on March 27 I made an impassioned plea and a protest to the president of the board, urging him to protect the spontaneity of the tests. I also suggested means of preventing the cowardice of copying. I am also determined to offer any assistance that you may require so that the examinations might be fair. What do you want: I am an idealist! (AM, pp. 97–98)

The letter to Professor Calabrese is even more ringing and explicit and shows how dismayed he was by the plagiarism. In it we read: "I am not acting out of pride, but because of an innate sense of justice. Woe to those who accuse me on this point! Will I be the victim? That does not matter, since I am a lesser light among so many brilliant stars, and I will be content to be eclipsed, provided that the bright stars are the ones that rise, and not some nebulous ninnies. I hope therefore that you will be so good as to prohibit the use of books or notes and to make sure of it" (AM, p. 99).

The competition finally was held, and, lo and behold, what Moscati feared came to pass: favoritism. A friend and colleague of his, who had no recommendation, was blatantly mistreated by the board. Moscati learned of it and immediately addressed such strong, resentful words to the president that the board was induced to correct its judgment. One can imagine, obviously, everyone's vexation and also the attitude of the president and of the board members toward the young doctor, who was a contestant too.

From various sources we know what happened after the board of examiners read Doctor Moscati's written examination. "The president himself, a renowned judge," as Professor Landolfi informs us, "having set aside all rancor, when confronted with such great erudition and so much genial knowledge, was the first to offer his congratulations amidst the enthusiastic applause of the contestants themselves and of the whole audience." (Ibid.)

Moscati's brother Eugenio testified: "When his scientific essay was read aloud, and he was invited to breach the anonymity imposed in the competition (the invitation came from the late Professor Cardarelli, a member of the board), he refused and was compelled by his colleagues, who triumphantly accompanied him back to his house.

Professor Cardarelli, on that occasion, said that in sixty years of teaching he had never run across a young man like him, and for the rest of his life he was very fond of him and had him as his attending physician" (PSV, §72).

The triumphant winner of the competition was then thirty-one years old, and his fame spread everywhere. In the Ospedale degli Incurabili "he was greeted as the victor", Professor Quagliariello recalls,

> amid the exultation of the patients, who already knew his great humanity, and of his colleagues, who had had to acknowledge his superiority, an acknowledgment that his modesty and affability had made particularly swift and easy. He took possession of his new post, and into the gray drabness of the ward entrusted to his care he immediately brought the warmth of his enthusiasm and the light of his faith. Groups of young students and young doctors began to gather around him and follow him from bed to bed as he visited the sick, eager to learn the secret of his art of diagnosing the most insidious maladies, sometimes with a rapidity and certainty that truly were somewhat miraculous. (GQ, pp. 92–93)

In addition to this activity, Moscati still worked at the Institute of Pathological Anatomy, of which he became the director in 1925. Furthermore, at the suggestion of Professor Cardarelli, he was appointed adjunct associate of the Royal Academy of Medicine and Surgery.

Still in 1911 he qualified as an adjunct professor of physiological chemistry, and the accrediting committee, in its report, after a detailed examination of his fourteen publications, rendered a favorable judgment, stating that "the candidate demonstrates excellent preparation for university teaching, since these are so many valuable original contributions to the solution of various important questions in this scientific field.... From the results of the teaching test, the committee is convinced that he also possesses the aptitudes to be able to teach effectively and successfully."[1]

Any comment on these commendations is superfluous. Moscati's scientific preparation was once again publicly and officially acknowledged, and the thirty-one-year-old professor had a brilliant career ahead of him.

---

[1] The report of the Panel of Judges is reprinted in F. D'Onofrio, *Giuseppe Moscati visto da un medico* (Naples: F. Giannini, 1987), 63–67.

5

Passing Up a Professorship

Upon winning first place in the 1911 competition, Moscati became fully involved in the work at the Ospedale degli Incurabili, yet at the same time he did not give up his scientific research and university teaching. In those days hospital physicians could offer instruction as adjunct university professors in the hospitals. Indeed, many great professors of medicine at that time came from a hospital setting.

In 1911, besides the titles that he had won, Moscati was an assistant professor of physiological chemistry, and in the academic year 1917–1918 he was called on by the faculty of medicine to replace Professor Filippo Bottazzi in the official course of physiology; in 1917–1918 and 1919–1920 he substitute-taught the course of physiological chemistry, while Bottazzi himself, who was director of the Institute of Physiology and then Grand Rector of the University, recommended him, together with Professor Quagliariello, for scientific research and experiments in the Institute of Physiological Chemistry.

In those years Moscati was well known in the medical world for his work as a contributor and editor of specialized academic journals, which were supported and directed by instructors who upheld the Neapolitan medical class. He wrote for the pages of *Folia medica*, *Nuova rivista clinico-terapeutica*, *Archivio di scienze biologiche*, *Giornale internazionale delle scienze mediche*, *Rinascenza medica*, *Atti dell'Accademia medico-chirurgica*, and for the magazine *La riforma medica*. In 1911, Professor Rummo suggested that he become the English- and German-language correspondent for the last-mentioned publication, since he had a very good command of both languages.

Between 1903, the year of his doctoral degree, and 1916, Moscati had a good twenty-seven scientific publications to his name.

With these achievements as a teacher and a scientist on his resume, why did Professor Moscati never hold a professorial chair? This question is all the more perplexing, given that many, many university instructors, such as Domenico Cotugno, Salvatore Tommasi and Antonio Cardarelli, came precisely from the Ospedale degli Incurabili.

Professor Gaetano Quagliariello gives us the answer, adding also particular details that concern him personally. "Whereas plans had to be made", he writes, "to fill the chair of physiological chemistry, which was vacant following the death of Professor Malerba, which had occurred in late 1917, and whereas the Faculty was leaning toward him, who had already taught those courses to the full satisfaction of both teachers and students during the long period of Malerba's illness and after his death, he informed them that he would not accept the position, and suggested and recommended my name; as a result, the position was conferred on me." And he continues: "How many of these generous gestures he performed is known to God alone; sometimes they remained unknown even to those who benefited from them" (GQ, p. 94).

Professor Quagliariello made the same statement during the cause for beatification. This remembrance exalts the figure of Moscati but also does honor to the man who thus testified explicitly to it. And Quagliariello (note well) was then Grand Rector of the University of Naples.

Still on the same subject, he adds:

> And Moscati performed another more painful act of self-denial, passing up the tenured professorship [*insegnamento ufficiale*] that he inevitably would have obtained if he had wanted it, and he did this for love of his hospital and of his students, who surrounded him in ever-increasing numbers. And perhaps also out of a desire to mortify an ambition that certainly must have smiled on his youth.... And so, free from all earthly ambition, he dedicated himself entirely, mind and heart, to his patients and to the education of young doctors. The hospital became his home, his love, his sanctuary. (Ibid.)

In light of these testimonies, all commentary becomes useless, and the esteem that we have for Moscati, the man of science, is transformed into due admiration and profound veneration. Only a noble soul, one moreover that was touched by God's grace and docile to the promptings of the Spirit, could attain such a spiritual height and direct his life toward such a great and sublime goal.

After this conscious and deliberate choice, Professor Moscati definitively opted for hospital work: to his hospital rounds he devoted his time, experience, human abilities and supernatural gifts. The patients, with their ailments and their physical and spiritual sufferings, were always uppermost in his thoughts, because "they are the faces of Jesus Christ, immortal, godlike souls, and the Gospel precept urges us to love them as ourselves."

These are the convictions that he always expresses in his writings, particularly when he addresses colleagues, whom he reminds that "suffering should be treated not as a twitch or a muscular contraction, but as the cry of a soul, to whom another brother, the doctor, runs with the ardent love of charity."

Obviously the fame of the master could not remain within the narrow walls of the lecture hall or in the hospital wards: everyone was talking about his lectures, his diagnostic gifts, his work among the sick. The Administrative Board of the Hospital for Incurables intervened officially and in 1919 appointed him director of the Third Men's Ward.

Worth remembering are the expressions that Moscati wrote on July 26, 1919, shortly after his appointment, to Senator Giuseppe D'Andrea, president of the Ospedali Riuniti of Naples:

> As a boy, I looked with interest at the Ospedale degli Incurabili, which my father pointed out to me in the distance from the terrace of our house, inspiring in me feelings of pity for the nameless suffering that was alleviated within those walls. A salutary dismay seized me, and I began to think of the transitory character of all things, and my illusions passed away, as the flowers fell from the orange groves that surrounded me. Then, being thoroughly occupied by my initial literary studies, I did not suspect and did not dream that, one day, in that white building, at whose windows could scarcely be distinguished, like white phantoms, the hospital

patients, I would one day hold a position at the top of the clinical hierarchy.... I will endeavor, with God's help, and with my insignificant powers, to live up to the trust that is placed in me, and to collaborate in the reconstruction of the old Neapolitan hospitals, which are so worthy on account of their charity and culture, but so poor today. (AM, pp. 110–111)

The Hospital for Incurables was bombarded in the Second World War, and today only a part of its former splendor remains. In Moscati's day it consisted of various buildings containing wards, galleries, lecture halls, corridors and study halls, and it was surrounded by gardens, cloistered enclosures and fountains. All of these locations were overflowing, not only with patients and inmates, but also with famous clinicians, assistants, nurses and young students. University courses were given there, taught by famous men of the stature of Leonardo Bianchi, Gaetano Rummo, Domenico Capozzi and Antonio Cardarelli.

Along with the adjacent church of Santa Maria del Popolo, the hospital boasts of very ancient origins, and in addition to being a house for medical care, it was a center of faith, piety and works of mercy.

In the late 1400s, in Italy and above all in Naples, after the death of Charles VIII of France, the so-called *mal francese* ("the French disease", that is, syphilis) began to spread, and those who were afflicted by it—and they were very numerous—were considered incurables. Christian charity immediately began to care for those poor unfortunates, and *lazzaretti* and hospices began to spring up everywhere. But the one who started the most famous hospital then, which was called specifically the "Hospital for Incurables" and still bears that name today, was a woman of Catalan origin, Maria Richeza, who with her husband Giovanni Longo had come to Naples in 1506 as part of the retinue of Ferdinand III, "the Catholic". The poor woman had become paralyzed after being poisoned by one of her maidservants during a banquet. She was cured after a pilgrimage to Loreto, and from then on there was no end to her charitable activity. She made the rounds of the many almshouses and hospitals, cared for the sick, treated them and sought to involve other women in her work.

A turning point in her life and her activity came in 1518 when she met a notary from Genoa, Don Ettore Vernazza, who was inspired by true charity and traveled around Italy promoting aid to the incurables. At first Signora Longa felt incapable of carrying out a grandiose project, but little by little other people became involved, plans were made and discussed at length, and on February 10, 1520, a contract was drawn up for the purchase of houses and gardens on the hill of Sant'Angelo, in the Montagna district [*sedile*], where the present-day Ospedale degli Incurabili then arose, which was destined to become the largest and most important hospital in Naples and in Southern Italy and one of the largest in Italy.

Despite her reluctance, Maria was appointed Rector or Governor of the Hospital, whereby most of the work conducted there fell on her shoulders: she had to supervise the admission and discharge of the inmates, organize the services and direct the activities.

In 1535 she founded the Third Order of St. Francis for women, or the Capuchinesses, which is still famous today in Naples under the name of the *Trentatré* [the "Thirty-three"].

God again sent trials to Signora Longo: her former paralysis returned and, after sixteen years of intense work, she left the Incurabili, having become a poor sick woman herself. She had the joy of being guided and sustained by Saint Gaetano Thiene and lived another seven years in the cloister among her sisters. She spent this period of her life in prayer and penance. Notwithstanding the disaster that struck the Capuchin Order as a result of the subversive theories of Don Juan de Valdés, she remained faithful to God and to the Church until her death, which occurred in 1552.

Over the years no less than twenty-five saints, blesseds and venerables were associated with the Ospedale degli Incurabili. Among them we should mention Saint Cajetan (1480–1547), Saint Alphonsus Maria de Liguori (1697–1787), Saint Jane Antide Thouret (1765–1826), Saint Caterina Volpicelli (1839–1892), Blessed Ludovico of Casoria (1814–1885), Blessed Bartolo Longo (1841–1926) and, last chronologically, Saint Giuseppe Moscati.

In the Hospital for Incurables Saint Giuseppe Moscati practiced his profession until his death, and above all practiced charity there in a heroic way.

6

Professor and Teacher of Spirituality

Even though he declined a professorial chair at the university, Moscati was always a professor and a teacher. He was professor and teacher of medical subjects, but through them he communicated his spirituality.

From the testimonies of his colleagues and students we know that he was particularly gifted as an instructor. He combined a serious, solid, basic preparation with the desire to update medical knowledge, a passion for research, an innate curiosity about new developments, and the ability to stroll through different areas of medicine, without encroaching on the fields of other specialists, yet understanding the scope thereof, examining their possibilities and taking account of their limits.

In addition to all this he had the ability to express himself and to communicate persuasively, together with a noble, dignified character and a particularly attractive physical appearance. The descriptions by some of his students, who later became famous physicians, leave us astonished and almost incredulous. No doubt his personality, his eyes and his manner emanated an influence that conquered and fascinated. Professor Enrico Polichetti, a renowned surgeon at the hospital in Venice and a former student of

Moscati, writes: "He had a graceful appearance, a somewhat slender build, rather tall in stature, a distinguished, direct personality, a refined character, noble comportment, lively features; the result was thus a harmonious whole. Certainly this too contributed to the fact that he was well regarded, well liked and even loved by the public. As for his physiognomy, with that oval face he was the sort of man who is usually called handsome, but in Naples is known as a 'distinguished nobleman': and he really was one in his mentality and in his actions."[1]

Doctor Alfonso Preziosi, a doctor in Avellino, remembers him as follows: "I still see before me, as many others do, the gentle, serene, affable, keen and charming look of our teacher who used to peer into our souls. He seemed to us to be 'the living oracle' who was constantly seeking the truth. He watched paternally over us students in our studies and hospital internships.... His gaze, which was always serene and charming, poured into us all, with wisdom, the treasures of his science, of his medical knowledge, of his humanity and the light of his soul and of the truth."[2]

We will omit other testimonials by his students, but we cannot fail to quote the one by Doctor Enrico Sica, who testified in the process of beatification of the Servant of God Giuseppe Moscati: "His learning in the most disparate branches of medical science, which is made up of around twenty specialized disciplines, was so complete in all its ramifications that those who were studying to be specialists

---

[1] E. Polichetti, "Giuseppe Moscati e la malattia mortale di Enrico Caruso", a lecture given at the L. Armanni Institute of the Ospedale degli Incurabili of Naples, reprinted in *La riforma medica* 17 (1956): 491.

[2] A. Preziosi, *Giuseppe Moscati, apostolo di scienza, fede e carità* (Avellino, 1978), 47.

found themselves calling on him constantly to ask him for clarifications. Amazing incidents often occurred in which he, against his will, was compelled to point out the way of truth to experienced specialists" (PSV, §643).

Doctor Sica continues:

> As for the diligence of the Servant of God as a teacher, one of his chief aims in life was his passion to transmit to others, as completely as possible, all the ideas that were the fruit of his knowledge and experience. I do not think that I exaggerate in saying that there is and can be no one at all to compare with his stature as a teacher, that is, as a learned man who educates. He made his hospital ward available to all who wished to practice; which of course prompted everyone to visit it assiduously. In his lectures he used to put it as follows: "I never present to you common clinical cases, because you have the leisure to observe these on the ward, where you can study them assiduously so as to follow their course. You know very well that I and my colleagues [he meant his assistants, whom he never described as such] are always at your disposal. Here we must discuss chiefly diseases that are rare or difficult to diagnose, because only in that way will you be able to bring a good preparation to your professional practice". (PSV, §649)

Not only students attended the lectures of Professor Moscati, but also "graduates, both young and old".

> And in that company there were older doctors, who during the war, which was then over, had been

high-ranking officers in the army medical corps (majors, lieutenant colonels, and so forth). That company, which was celebrated in the memories of the orderlies, nurses and sisters of that time, was like a new institution in the hospital setting. Some individuals of that company felt so attracted by the new teacher that they spared no effort or trouble to obtain permission from the Administration of the [United] Hospitals to remain in those departments following the maestro, even outside of lecture hours. So it was that the number of volunteer medical assistants increased; wearing white jackets and crowded around the Servant of God, they formed as it were a new company of charity that was entirely devoted to the study and assistance of the sick. (PSV, §§209–11)

These words are from the deposition of Professor Mario Mazzeo, a colleague of Moscati.

A friend of the family, Alberto Sorrentino, the first honorary president of the Court of Appeals, informs us of two special traits of the professor: his prudence and his tact.

In teaching, he never supported ideas or scientific theories that were too adventurous. Indeed, I recall that once while reading the *Revista medica* he said: "These folks too often rush to make judgments and decisions about drugs or diseases, as the case may be. Experience is necessary." When occasionally a student made some blunder in scientific teaching, he prudently would not rebuke and correct him directly, but as the opportunity presented itself he started a discussion or made remarks about the subject in which the student had erred, and so by speaking generally to the whole student body he corrected the error. (PSV §§838–39)

Another feature of Moscati's professorial activity was his expertise in performing autopsies. For him, autopsies were always lectures, and his students still recall with admiration his diligence, expertise and profound competence. As was mentioned, he had been working for years in the Institute of Pathological Anatomy, and in 1925 he had agreed to become its director. He excelled in this field and made use of the autopsies that he performed to educate his students professionally. Professor Quagliariello considered him "a true master in performing autopsies".

The late Doctor Renato Guerrieri, head physician at the Ospedale degli Incurabili, who died in Naples on May 6, 2001, assisted by Doctor Antonio Salvio, who presently [2004] still works in the same hospital, through persistent, detailed research in the archives, which were partially destroyed in the bombardments of the Second World War, managed to bring to light several reports of post-mortem examinations and clinical histories written in Professor Moscati's own hand or signed by him. "Almost certainly," Doctor Guerrieri declares, "these are 'exemplary' clinical histories for the students, or clinical histories serving as the 'basis' for his lectures."

Professor Raffaele Rossiello, who has studied the pathological anatomy of Saint Giuseppe Moscati competently and in depth, says that after the saint's death, neither the medical journals, nor publications that commemorated him with various speeches, nor even the numerous biographies gave prominence "to his activity as an expert coroner and director of the Luciano Armanni Institute of

Pathological Anatomy and Histology.... The rediscovery
of a register of the autopsies performed by Moscati in the
period between December 25, 1925, and February 9, 1927,
however, brings to our attention once again this hitherto
little-known aspect of the complex medical and scientific
personality of Giuseppe Moscati."[3]

It should be noted that one autopsy record bears the
date July 25, 1926, Moscati's birthday!

The anatomical ward, obviously, is a sad, desolate spot,
and Professor Moscati understood very well that only a
symbol of faith could bring a breath of life to a place where
death seemed triumphant. And what symbol could better
bring that breath of life than the crucifix, which contains
suffering and hope? Moscati's first biographer, Archbishop
Ercolano Marini, reports what he wrote to Doctor Andrea
Pirro, the professor's assistant:

> One day while we were visiting the patients on the
> ward, we were invited to go to the autopsy room. We
> were surprised by the invitation and unable to explain
> the reason for it, since we knew that there were no
> autopsies to be performed that day. Professor Moscati,
> though, from whom the invitation had come, had
> already set out, and we hurried to follow him. On the
> anatomical table we found nothing, and those who
> had arrived before us were looking up intently at the
> opposite wall, on which they were admiring a crucifix
> that the professor had had someone place there, with
> the inscription beneath it: *"Ero mors tua, o mors."*

[3] R. Rossiello, *L'anatomia patologica di san Giuseppe Moscati* (Messina: Esur,
1992), 7.

["O death, I will be your death." (Douay-Rheims)]
We had been invited to pay homage to Christ, the Life
who was returning to that place of death after too long
an absence![4]

The profoundly Christian mind of Professor Moscati
had brought life "to a place of death". And this breath
of life was noticed, because "at the beginning of every
autopsy," Professor Mazzeo recalls, "the Servant of God,
before getting ready to take up the tools and use them,
took a long, meaningful look at the crucifix and then at
the cadaver.... He often ended with this remark: 'This is
what we are: riches, revelries, honors, hatreds, and then....
How instructive death is!'" (PSV, §218).

---

[4] E. Marini, *Il professor Giuseppe Moscati della Regia Università di Napoli* (Naples: F. Giannini, 1929), 153–54. The Crucifix with the ornamental scroll on which the above-cited verse from the book of the Prophet Hosea (13:14) is written, is preserved in the Moscati archives in the Rectory of the Gesù Nuovo in Naples.

7

Extraordinary Clinical Intuition

In Moscati's days, in the 1920s, medicine had not made the advances that we take for granted today. It was rather artisanal, since effective diagnostic methods, laboratory equipment and precise high-tech instruments did not exist. The doctor often relied on his experience, his personal intuition, his skill. Moscati had experience, intuition and skill—gifts that his colleagues and students noticed every day.

The above-cited Professor Enrico Polichetti, recalling the years he spent under Moscati's direction, wrote:

> Indeed, those were still the days in which our profession was more art than science, largely dependent, especially in surgery, on personal virtuosity, individuality, and the natural gifts of just one person, refined and perfected with experience, rather than on collaboration, research and laboratory work. But in both respects he was the most complete, the most up-to-date of all the Neapolitan clinicians of that time.

Moscati, following the teachings of Neapolitan medicine, attributed great importance to visits and conversation with the patient and to the symptoms that he managed to perceive. In addition he kept abreast of new developments and followed Italian and foreign-language publications, both books and scientific journals. He spoke French, English and German well and was editor of the journal *La riforma medica* for foreign literature.

Despite their knowledge, diligence and conscientiousness, since they lacked the diagnostic equipment that is widely available to modern medicine, as was noted, healthcare professionals were compelled to refine their intuition as a means of helping the patient. Obviously, the results were not always optimal, but intuition was an indispensable aid to the physician. He was like a blind man, obliged to compensate for his lack of sight by his other senses.

By unanimous acclaim, Professor Moscati was endowed with extraordinary intuition. Often his diagnoses caused consternation but, after the results, that consternation turned into amazement and admiration. Sometimes a critic, envious of Moscati's successes and fame, dared to criticize him and to speak ill of his daring diagnoses, but he had to surrender to the factual evidence and acknowledge Dr. Moscati's superiority.

Here is how Doctor Soccorso Tecce remembers it: "he was endowed with vast erudition and a clinical intuition that had something divine about it; he formulated diagnoses that were so complex in nature and *in situ* that, if a post-mortem examination had not confirmed them, they would have appeared to be rash."[1]

This judgment is repeated by Doctor Enrico Sica, a former student of Moscati, who in his long deposition for the process of canonization declared:

[1] E. Marini, *Il professor Giuseppe Moscati della Regia Università di Napoli* (Naples: F. Giannini, 1929), 152.

Amazing incidents often occurred in which he, against his will, was compelled to point out the way of truth to experienced specialists. We, who listened to his lectures every day, continually had the opportunity to observe and verify such incidents, which set the medical faculty in Naples abuzz, all the more so given the fact that in all sorts of ways he sought unassailable verification for the diagnosis that he had formulated. For instance when there had been no surgeon's hand to bring the truth to light or a laboratory investigation or an X ray or other specialized test to document whether or not the judgment that he had formulated was accurate. (PSV, §657)

Enrico Caruso's illness

His students and assistants relate other incidents, but the situation in which Moscati most dramatically proved his diagnostic ability was the illness of the tenor Enrico Caruso, who in the final phase of his life, after various useless medical consultations in America, had disembarked in Naples and taken up lodgings in the Hotel Tramontano in Sorrento.

Moscati, summoned from Naples, visited him in late July of 1921, performed an exploratory puncture and diagnosed a "subphrenic abscess". No other American or Italian physician, among them Professor Cardarelli himself, had taken into consideration the cause that Moscati, in contrast, declared with certainty.

Information concerning Moscati's visit to the great tenor Caruso is provided to us by Professor Polichetti, a student of Moscati, who in the journal *La Riforma medica* (vol. 17 dated April 28, 1956), in seven densely-written pages, published the conference that he gave to the L. Armanni Institute of the Ospedale degli Incurabili in Naples, in which he portrays an exceptional "physician" and "apostle" and "clarifies the sad episode that deprived Italy and the lyric art of the greatest tenor of all time". Professor Polichetti writes:

In the biweekly *Annali Ravasini* dated February 1, 1955, no. 3, appeared an interesting but inaccurate article entitled: "How Caruso Died", in which the cause of the tenor's death is attributed, erroneously, to "a common purulent pleurisy" that was diagnosed too late—due to the carelessness and negligence of his personal physician, Dorothy Benjamin, whom he had recently married, and a botched operation in New York; it adds that Caruso, after returning to Italy with "the condition terribly advanced", did not submit soon enough to an unspecified new operation, which Professor Raffaele Bastianelli of Rome had called for, after visits and consultations by senior representatives of the medical faculty in Naples.

The episode stirred up a great deal of public opinion and caused something of a furor.... A cartoon in the weekly *Monsignor Perrelli* depicted the cemetery in Naples and caricatures of the Neapolitan medical luminaries at the time, among them the head of the great Antonio Cardarelli, with the caption, "We too, by our mistakes, but without being Americans, helped to populate Poggioreale." Caruso had just been buried there a few days previously.

Polichetti then speaks about the exceptional figure of Professor Moscati, and continues:

> It has come to my knowledge, as his student, that Professor Giuseppe Moscati, in late July 1921, had visited Enrico Caruso for the first time at the Hotel Tramontano in Sorrento; the tenor had already had an operation in America for purulent pleurisy without being cured; Moscati diagnosed a subphrenic abscess, which had remained undiagnosed until then, confirming this by the extraction of pus through a puncture in the subdiaphragmatic region. But he found the patient failing rapidly and in a worrisome general septic state, and therefore little or nothing could be done.
>
> In fact Caruso, having started a journey from Sorrento on August 1, took a turn for the worse, and while waiting to make a connection to Rome, stopped in Naples and died there on the morning of August 2, 1921, in the Hotel Vesuvio on the Via Partenope. The teacher himself immediately related all this to us students, and in his lectures on the subject, in later years, he sometimes mentioned it for the purpose of instruction! Moreover the fact, which had become public knowledge in the city of Naples, was the talk of all Italy and abroad, even across the ocean, given the fame of the singer and the accusations against the doctors, most of them foreign [that is, non-Italian].
>
> While conversing with one of the most distinguished Italian anatomical pathologists, who holds a chair in Padua (Professor Mario Raso), who at that time was in Brazil, he reported to me that there had been a lot of

talk, even there, about the unexpected death of Caruso and the brilliant, exact diagnosis by Moscati, who had been consulted too late. He had also heard Professor E. Berger confirm this while taking his course in medical semiotics [symptomatology] in Naples.

Polichetti mentions other names, among them Professor Vincenzo Tramontano, director of the Institute of Pathological Anatomy and Histology of the United Hospitals of Naples. "Moreover," he notes, "Professor Tramontano, for the record, reminded me also about the modest fee received by the maestro for that famous consultation, for the exploratory puncture, the expense of the trip to Sorrento and the subsequent visit in Naples—two thousand lire all told." Then he continues:

The accuracy of his diagnosis (after so many doubts of others), of the site of the sample, and of the fatal prognosis, along with the indication that a surgical intervention was necessary, for the sole purpose of attempting to save the patient, given the seriousness of his condition and the generalized sepsis (although it could not be performed), increased more and more the popularity and reputation that Moscati already enjoyed universally.... His keen, lively, versatile mind had an intuition—the malevolent and the envious called it caprice—a marvelous power of penetration and synthesis: he saw and immediately grasped the strangest situations, collated the most varied, distant and disparate facts, utilizing them for a clinical diagnosis, since everything spoke to him a language that was often not commonly understood.

Besides the quotations taken from the article by Professor Polichetti, allow me to reprint another that reports several very significant incidents.

In an elderly rural chief of surgery, Professor A.S. Veneto, who for years had suffered from incurable pains in his hands, he discovered an unknown case of syphilis after being consulted by him while he was a refugee in Naples during World War I; the diagnosis was based solely on the fact that the pains stopped when his hands were immersed in solutions of corrosive sublimate [an antiseptic]; an enthusiastic admirer of the maestro, he consulted him also for his heart problems and kept a very grateful memory of him alive in Venice.

Based on a thoracic-abdominal cyanosis and a metallic odor in the mouth of a persistent glutton and drunkard—a fat, thick-set forty-year-old farmer from Solopaca who was vomiting blood massively and therefore died soon after—who was brought to him for an emergency consultation by the Aceto brothers, he diagnosed an acute case of hemorrhagic pancreatitis without gastro-duodenal ulcers. With the swiftness of his wingèd thought, on his first meeting with the patient, he applied, vertically, to his mesogastrium [the region of the abdomen surrounding the navel] two stethoscopes, the diaphragms of which oscillated due to the pulsation transmitted from the aorta, which was compressed by the extravasation of pancreatic blood. In fact, at the autopsy, which I saw him perform, the pancreas was crushed by a bloody mass that invaded the whole retroperitoneal region on that side, with a notable congestion of the stomach and the duodenum, the mucus of which was infarcted with blood coming from the hemorrhages by rexis, which also filled the gastro-intestinal contents. Despite the diffidence and contrary opinion of others, he diagnosed *in vita* [while the patient was alive] a tuberculosis of the heart, which was confirmed precisely by the post-mortem examination.

The assistants and students of Professor Moscati were enthusiastic admirers of the maestro and spoke frequently about his intuition, reporting facts that they had witnessed. To represent them all, we recall just one of them, related by Doctor Michele Farano, an ex-medical officer:

> In the late twenties and early thirties, I was a boy and often went with my parents to Vibonati (Salerno), my birthplace, bordering on Sapri, to the house of my maternal grandparents, where my grandmother and my three uncles were still living. My Uncle Federico told me that he had an attack of hemoptysis [expectoration of blood] and was taken by Doctor Biaggio Vecchio, the family physician, to Naples for a medical consultation with a specialist, Professor Giuseppe Moscati. When they arrived at the palazzo where Professor Moscati resided, they did not find him at home and waited in front of the gate. When Professor Moscati arrived, they took the elevator and Dr. Vecchio began to tell Professor Moscati that my uncle had had an attack of "tubercular hemoptysis", since at that time "tuberculosis" was rather widespread in Italy, and whenever a case of hemoptysis was observed, it was usually diagnosed as tuberculosis. In

the elevator, Professor Moscati immediately responded to Dr. Vecchio's words: "Is this the face of a tubercular patient? He has a pulmonary abscess on the right hemithorax." Without yet having examined my uncle, Professor Moscati made the diagnosis of "pulmonary abscess" and specified "on the right hemithorax". That is an amazing feat!

In fact, as treatment for my Uncle Federico, Professor Moscati prescribed that he eat garlic, because at that time antibiotics had not yet been discovered; his pulmonary abscess emptied through the anterior wall of the right hemithorax, into which the pus from the pulmonary abscess had drained, and he was completely cured. In those days garlic was used as a medicine for bronchopulmonary infections. Indeed, it is well known that eighty percent of the garlic that is ingested concentrates in the lungs, like alcohol. That is why an odor of garlic or of alcohol is emitted with each breath of a person who has ingested it.[2]

After these accounts we are left astounded and in awe, but let us not forget that Moscati was a man like any other and therefore limited even in the talents by which he excelled. His diligence and conscientiousness in practicing his profession were great, but sometimes insufficient.

"Consequently," Professor Mario Mazzeo testified, "many times, in extremely difficult cases, he devoted himself to prayer with greater intensity" (PSV, §368).

---

[2] Cf. *Il Gesù Nuovo*, periodical of the House and the church of the Jesuit Fathers and of the Opera San Giuseppe Moscati (1996): 1:26.

8

Man of Science, Man of Faith

John Paul II, in the Encyclical *Fides et ratio*, published on
September 14, 1998, writes:

> In the field of scientific research, a positivistic mentality
> took hold which not only abandoned the Christian
> vision of the world, but more especially rejected every
> appeal to a metaphysical or moral vision. It follows that
> certain scientists, lacking any ethical point of reference,
> are in danger of putting at the centre of their concerns
> something other than the human person and the
> entirety of the person's life. Further still, some of these,
> sensing the opportunities of technological progress,
> seem to succumb not only to a market-based logic, but
> also to the temptation of a quasi-divine power over
> nature and even over the human being. (no. 46)

These painful observations of the Pope concerning
our era can be applied without the slightest doubt to
the first decades of the past century: the years in which
Moscati lived and practiced his profession. Those were
years dominated by positivism and materialism, in which
a pseudoscientific crisis drove many people away from

God and from the Church, as though true science were incompatible with the supernatural, and technology could satisfy the highest aspirations of the human heart. It was a revival of the ancient error and pretense of building an exclusively earthly city, where there was no room for God: either he was ignored or people thought that they could do without him.

Giuseppe Moscati, who had received and imbibed from his parents a lively faith and a religiosity sustained by prayer and trust in God, went against the current and always directed his life and his work toward higher goals. From boyhood and then during his years of study he had remained faithful to the teachings of his family, increasing and never diminishing his love for the Lord.

Since he was at the height of his career, both in university teaching and in his hospital work, he was admired and emulated for his scientific knowledge, but no less so for his faith and the supernatural vision with which he treated illnesses. And this vision was precisely what gave him his just assessment of human knowledge and, in many cases, the humility to be able to recognize its limits. "And then what can we other doctors do?" he wrote on February 8, 1923, to his former student Giuseppe Napolitano. "Very little! And therefore, being unable to help the body, let us help the soul, and when dealing with unfortunate cases, let us remember our duties of the spirit that proceed from the faith of our fathers."

To a former student, Doctor Agostino Consoli, from Lagonegro (Potenza), who in Naples had attended his clinical instructions and, upon completing his course of specialization, sent him a note of thanks, Moscati replied with a letter that is a genuine plan of life. In a few phrases the maestro sums up for the student extraordinarily lofty moral sentiments and convictions:

Naples, July 22, 1922

I thank you cordially for your letter: I have done only very little for my young colleagues, but my meager strength did not allow me to do more!

Although you are now far away, do not stop cultivating and reviewing your medical knowledge every day. Progress is found in a continual critique of what we have learned. Only one science is unshakable and unshaken, the one revealed by God, the science of the hereafter!

In all your works, look to Heaven, and to the eternity of life and of the soul, and then you will have a very different orientation from the one that merely human considerations would suggest to you, and your work will be inspired for the better. I wish you every success.

I kiss you. Your very affectionate Giuseppe Moscati

(AM, pp. 370–71)

To another former assistant of his in the Third Men's Ward, Doctor Antonio Guerricchio, who would later be the head physician and director of the City Hospital of Matera, he wrote on July 22, 1922, responding to a thank-you letter. After expressing his grief over the unfair treatment that his former students often received at the hands of those whom he calls "the priests of science", he turns to a higher perspective and shows his friend the true assessment of human science, which is valid only if it can be joined with charity, the virtue capable of transforming the world. Interesting too is the expression of friendship and the joy that he experienced at the thought of having conveyed a spiritual message. All this was for him a sublime task to be accomplished only with supernatural help.

> Not science but charity has transformed the world, in some eras; and only very few men have gone down in history because of their science; but all men can remain imperishable, a symbol of eternal life, in which death is only a stage, a metamorphosis for the sake of a higher ascent, if they dedicate themselves to doing good.
>
> In my heart there is still a keen regret, knowing that you are far away; the only thing that consoles me is that you have preserved within yourself something of me; not because it is worth anything, but because of that spiritual message that I strove to uphold and spread around: a sublime task, but so unattainable with my meager strength. (AM, p. 248)

As we see from these two letters and from many others, Moscati, as an established professional, never confined himself to the narrow circle of human efforts, but was able to lift his sights to higher considerations and to strike a balance that allowed him to be open to suffering, to human miseries, to the poor and to the values of friendship. Human truth and divine truth come from a single source: from God, who is infinite truth.

In his vision of life, the initial words of the above-cited Encyclical *Fides et ratio* are marvelously borne out: "Faith and reason are like two wings on which the human spirit rises to the contemplation of truth; and God has placed in the human heart a desire to know the truth—in a word, to know himself—so that, by knowing and loving God, men and women may also come to the fullness of truth about themselves."

The concept of the union between science and faith cropped up not only in his writings; it must have been so common in his work that all who spoke about him noticed it in particular.

Professor Nicola Donadio stated: "Often I had the sense that his company, being at his side, immediately made everything better; that a conversation with him, even though it may have been very short, suddenly brought everything into a lofty, serene spiritual setting."[1]

A friend and colleague of Moscati, Professor Michele Landolfi, in a conference given on May 29, 1927, recalls that "there is no counting the troops of students who came to him, above all some doctors who recognized in him, as opposed to others, the true master." Then he asks: "What is the explanation for such dazzling, resounding success?"

Of course, there is no denying his inexhaustible erudition, his downright encyclopedic culture, springing from unattainable sources such as those of the Nile were at one time. Certainly, being outstanding in medicine and chemistry, he accomplished great things at the patient's bedside and in the laboratory, renewing the annals of the glorious "Luciano Armanni" Institute of Pathological Anatomy, but he was above all a man of faith.

[1] E. Marini, *Il professor Giuseppe Moscati della Regia Università di Napoli* (Naples: F. Giannini, 1929), 170.

Peppino Moscati was religious in the purest sense of the word, and as a doctor, a clinician and an instructor, he always demonstrated his fervent religiosity.

Every morning he could be seen, together with his many disciples, in the Church of the Gesù, performing the duties of a good Christian, and always and everywhere he was willing and able to make these sentiments of his prevail.... Wherever the spirit predominates over matter, there is victory! That explains the phenomenon! That is the answer to the question at the outset! (GM, pp. 134–35)

Faith, which was present in Professor Moscati no less than science, was the result of a personal conviction and a profound experience of life. Suffering had knocked several times at his door, and by accepting it in a Christian way, he was able to channel it. He had accepted with a supernatural spirit the death of his father and of his brother Alberto, and with Christian resignation he had witnessed the departure of his mother when he, already an established physician, had been able to do very little to prolong her life.

A very important idea is expressed in a letter of condolence to a friend, a lawyer by the name of Mariconda, who had lost his sister: "Life is an instant; honors, triumphs, riches and knowledge fail, before the fulfillment of the cry of Genesis, the cry flung by God against guilty man: 'You shall die!' But life does not end with death, it continues in a better world. To everyone has been promised, after the redemption of the world, the day that will reunite us with our dear departed ones, and that will bring us back to the supreme Love!" (AM, p. 274).

To Signorina Carlotta Petravella, too, whose mother had died, he wrote, among other things:

I tell you with conviction that your mother did not leave you and your sisters: she is watching over her children invisibly, now that she has experienced, in a better world, the mercy of God and is praying and asking for consolation and resignation for those who mourn her on earth. I too, as a boy, lost my father, and then, as an adult, my mother. And my father and mother are beside me; I sense their pleasant company; and if I seek to imitate them, who were just, I have their encouragement, and if I do something wrong, I have their good inspirations, as once during their lifetime I had their spoken counsels.

I understand your anguish and that of your sisters; it is the first true sorrow, and the first time that our dreams are shattered; it is the first call of your thoughts as a young woman to the realities of the world. But life has been described as a flash of lightning in eternity. That is our humanity. Because of the merit of the suffering that permeates it. The suffering that satiated the One who was clothed in our flesh and transcends matter and leads us to hope for happiness beyond this world. Blessed are those who follow this lead of the conscience and look "to the hereafter", where the earthly affections that seem to be prematurely broken off will be restored. (AM, p. 276)

Finally, we cannot neglect to recall the short but important letter that he sent from Lecce to the notary De Magistris, his dear friend, on the occasion of the death of his daughter. Besides sentiments and human emotions, Moscati also expresses his ideas of faith and is able to lift his sights, as he always did, to the vision of God. He reminds his friend of his daughter's devotion (which he had inculcated) to then-Blessed Thérèse of the Child Jesus.

Naples, March 7, 1924

Dear Sir,

I have here on my desk, among the first flowers of spring, the portrait of your daughter, and I pause, while I write, to meditate on the transitory nature of human things! Beauty and every charm of this life passes.... The only thing that remains eternally is love, the cause of every good work, which outlives us, which is our hope and our religion, because God is love. Satan sought to defile earthly love too, but God purified it through death. Majestic death which is not the end but the beginning of the sublime and the divine, compared to which these flowers and beauty are nothing!

May your little angel, snatched away in the freshness of her youth, like her beloved friend, whom she met again in recent days, Blessed Thérèse, help you and her mother from heaven and may she pray and care for you and protect and thank you.

Yours truly, with the most sincere gratitude,

Gius. Moscati (AM, pp. 284–85)

At the end of the Encyclical *Fides et ratio*, John Paul II turns to theologians and recommends that they always keep in mind "the words of that great master of thought and spirituality, Saint Bonaventure, who in introducing his *Itinerarium Mentis in Deum* invites the reader to recognize the inadequacy of 'reading without repentance, knowledge without devotion, research without the impulse of wonder, prudence without the ability to surrender to joy, action divorced from religion, learning sundered from love, intelligence without humility, study unsustained by divine grace, thought without the wisdom inspired by God'" (no. 105).

In these words of Saint Bonaventure, written seven centuries ago, we find, so to speak, the negative of a photograph of Saint Giuseppe Moscati. In the holy doctor, indeed, the fundamental points of Christian life identified by the Franciscan saint were completely reconciled and perfectly synthesized.

Paul VI, in the homily at the Mass for the beatification of Giuseppe Moscati (November 16, 1975), described him as follows: "a highly educated scientist, renowned for his scientific contributions at the international level, for his publications and journeys, for his insightful, sure diagnoses, for his bold, far-seeing interventions"! But even before that, in the same homily, he is presented in this way: "He is a layman who made his life a mission that was accomplished with evangelical authenticity, applying magnificently the talents that he had received from God. He is a physician, who made his profession the arena for an apostolate, a mission of charity, a means of lifting himself up and of winning over others to Christ the Savior! He is a university professor who left among his students a wake of profound admiration not only for his superb erudition, but also and especially for his example of moral rectitude, interior purity, and absolute self-denial that he gave from the lectern!"

We wish to conclude this chapter on the synthesis of science and faith in Moscati by citing a few thoughts of Father Agostino Gemelli, the founder and grand rector of the University of the Sacred Heart in Milan, and taken from an essay about the saintly physician that was published less than three years after his death, in 1930:

> The phenomenon of a perfect and deliberate fusion of the Christian, the scientist and the man, which unfortunately is rare enough among those who are erudite in the medical sciences, is realized in Giuseppe Moscati. Those watertight compartments by means of which some minds forbid any intercommunication whatsoever between the raw realities of scientific research and the speculations of thought and the teachings of faith did not exist at all for him, who in his acknowledgment that God is the author of the material order and of the supernatural order had found the means of achieving a harmony between science and faith. This conviction was so profoundly rooted in Giuseppe Moscati that it was as plain as the sun, and not a single doubt darkened it, not even slightly.[2]

Father Gemelli is struck, moreover, by Moscati's remark: "The sick are the face of Christ", and by the crucifix placed in the anatomical ward, "where", he said, "the maestro sought confirmation for a diagnosis from the autopsy." He continues:

[2] A. Gemelli, "Una esemplare figura di medico cristiano", *Vita e Pensiero* (1930): 225.

In the face of the brutal reality of death, his faith exalts the pious image of the one who conquered it.... His diagnostic intuition is so sure and keen that his students and colleagues wonder whether they were not confronting a prodigious power of divination, and more than one even goes so far as to express the suspicion that in many cases he was enlightened by the Lord. A suspicion that is all too eloquent, because it does not notice that here we are on the threshold of a mystery in which human science, thoroughly imbued by faith and charity, seems to receive otherworldly reflections from on high.[3]

3 Ibid., 229.

9

Love for Christ and the Virgin Mary

Giuseppe Moscati was canonized by Pope John Paul II on October 25, 1987. At that time, from October 1 to 25, the Seventh General Assembly of the Synod of Bishops was being held in Rome on the topic of "The Vocation and Mission of the Lay Faithful in the Church and in the World", twenty years after the conclusion of the Second Vatican Council.

You could not have asked for a better coincidence: Giuseppe Moscati was a layman who had carried out in a Christian manner his mission in the Church and in the world. In the homily during the Mass of canonization, the Pope clearly stated: "The man whom from now on we will invoke as a saint of the universal Church appears to us as a concrete realization of the ideal of the Christian layman. Giuseppe Moscati, head physician of a hospital, a renowned researcher, a university instructor of human physiology and physiological chemistry, performed his many and various tasks with all the commitment and seriousness that the practice of these delicate lay professions requires."[1]

---

[1] *Acta Apostolicae Sedis, Acta Ioannis Pauli PP. II*, 594.

Where did Moscati get the strength and the courage to exemplify "the ideal of the Christian layman"? The Pontiff himself tells us in the same homily:

> In his constant relationship with God, Moscati found the light to understand better and to diagnose diseases and the warmth to be able to be a good neighbor to those who were suffering and expected the physician to serve them with sincere concern.
>
> From this profound, constant reference to God he drew the strength that sustained him and enabled him to live with integrity, honesty and absolute rectitude in his own delicate and complex setting, without reaching any sort of compromise.[2]

One day Moscati, in response to Signorina Emilia Pavese, who witnessed his intense work in the hospital and asked him where he got such strength, quoted the words of Saint Paul: "I can do all things in him who strengthens me" (Phil 4:13).

He encountered the Lord in his daily prayer: in the long time that he dedicated to it he was filled with Christ, whom he was then able to see in the sick and the needy. From the window of his little office he saw the apse of the Church of the Gesù Nuovo, and from the first rays of dawn he had a conversation with the Lord that gave him strength over the course of the day: in his hospital rounds, during his university lectures, in his conversations with his students and friends.

Many of those who knew him remember him kneeling before the Blessed Sacrament in the Churches of the

2 Ibid., 595.

Gesù Nuovo or Santa Chiara, particularly in the morning, before going to the hospital. "As for his devotion to the Most Holy Eucharist," Doctor Enrico Sica testified, "it has come to my knowledge that the Servant of God received Holy Communion daily, always preparing well and making a thanksgiving afterward. In church he maintained great recollection and devotion. During the elevation he remained kneeling, in profound adoration" (PSV, §677).

And the lawyer Nicola Mastelloni testified: "In his devotional practices, such as hearing Mass, receiving Holy Communion, or adoring the Most Blessed Sacrament, he gave signs of such devotion and recollection as to make clearly evident the great love that he had for God" (ibid., §927).

We have two more testimonies by persons who were very close to the saint, knew his habits and above all had a certain familiarity with him. The first is Signorina Emma Picchillo, a woman of profound spirituality, who had lived almost all her life at the Shrine of Pompei and was very close to Bartolo Longo. She knew the Moscati family well and was especially much liked by our saint and by his sister Nina. During the process of beatification she testified, among other things:

> The Servant of God had a special devotion to Jesus in the Blessed Sacrament. As far as I know, he received Communion every day and many times at a great sacrifice. Indeed, since he visited the sick outside of Naples too, upon returning from those visits, late in the day, he used to go into a church and receive Communion. I observed this four times in the Shrine

of Pompei, when he returned from Amalfi, Salerno, Campobasso, where he had gone to visit the sick. In this connection he told me: "What sweetness I experience in receiving Communion at the feet of our Lady! It seems to me that I become littler and I tell her things as they are". (Ibid., §476)

The Jesuit Father Giovanni Aromatisi had been on familiar terms with Professor Moscati for several years, knew his everyday habits well and was his spiritual director. In the process he testified, "He used to go to our Church of the Gesù for his devotional practices. Many times he heard and served my Mass" (ibid., §948).

After speaking about his friend's virtues, he continues:

As for his devotion to the Most Blessed Sacrament, that was the center of his whole life. He went to Communion every day and very often at very great inconvenience; and he used to travel at night fasting so as to be able to receive Holy Communion the next day. Word got around among his patients, especially those who lived far away, in Sicily and in Calabria, that if they wanted a visit from Professor Moscati, they would have to fetch the priest right away, so that he might be able to hear Mass, serving it, and go to Communion. Even if this had not been arranged previously, he went to Communion in whatever church he found open, however late it might be". (Ibid., §§ 954–55)

Moscati's concern about never missing Mass and about receiving the Eucharist is attested by other acquaintances of his by their personal recollections.

Professor Guido Piccinino, instructor of medical radiology at the University of Naples and a former student and then an assistant of the saint, testified:

> He urged his students to receive the sacraments, while leaving them completely free, and although he very often recommended the regular reception of Holy Communion, he did so only with persons who were close to him, whose religious education he knew about. In this connection I recall that once, when we had to go together to the Valle di Pompei to visit the founder, Bartolo Longo, now deceased, since he was supposed to give him a treatment, on the preceding day the Servant of God wrote me a lovely note in which he urged me to do us the pleasure of receiving Holy Communion together in the Shrine of Pompei the following day. And he wrote to me in that letter in precisely these words: "Since we have to go to the Valle di Pompei tomorrow, would you like to do us the pleasure of receiving Communion in the Shrine there? If so, remember to fast." (Ibid., §§ 82–83)

Professor Filippo Bottazzi, having learned that Moscati had to travel to the province of Lecce, invited him to stop at his villa in Diso. The saint went there and stayed for two days. The first morning Bottazzi, knowing his friend's habits, had the pastor celebrate Mass in the little chapel adjoining his house, but he forgot to tell him to return the following day. "But he remedied the situation rather simply", Bottazzi recalled. "The following morning, unbeknownst to everyone, he rose early and went, alone, to Diso to hear the first Mass, which a priest of that town celebrates in time for the farmers to go into the fields. We were all astounded by it."[3]

In the depositions for the process of beatification, many, in recalling Moscati's devotion to the Eucharist, spoke also about his love for Christ Crucified and for the Sacred Heart.

Loving Christ, Moscati could not help cherishing a special love for the Virgin Mary. There are many testimonies to this effect, and we must be content to cite only a few of the more important ones.

Doctor Orsi sums up this special devotion of his friend as follows:

> The Servant of God had the utmost devotion to our Lady, especially under the title of Our Lady of Good Counsel. Every day he recited the Holy Rosary and other devotions in honor of her, and on the occasions of the various feasts of the Blessed Virgin he did not fail to say special prayers and to attend the Divine Offices. It has come to my knowledge also, as I already mentioned before, that he had a great devotion to Our Lady of Pompei; to the Blessed Virgin under the title of Our Lady of Good Counsel he had—as I said—a special devotion, and I should think that he dedicated his vow of chastity to her, which he then observed in such an edifying way until his death. To the sick and to his students he used to talk about the Mother of God, seeking every occasion to exalt her greatness and to inculcate a special devotion to her. (PSV, §§ 764–65)

[3] E. Marini, *Il professor Giuseppe Moscati della Regia Università di Napoli* (Naples: F. Giannini, 1929), 180.

Our Lady was uppermost in his thoughts. He spoke about her frequently, carried his rosary in his waistcoat pocket and often fingered the beads and kissed it. At the sound of the Angelus bell he made the Sign of the Cross and invited those present in the hospital to recite the Angelus. The Hospital of Incurables still preserves a marble statue of the Madonna that he used to venerate in his department. On the table of his bedroom, on the other hand, he had a little bronze statue that depicts Mary and the Child asleep on her lap. She makes a sign to be quiet with her finger at her lips, obviously referring to the sleeping baby. The title is indicated underneath: *Vierge au silence* (French for "The Virgin of silence").[4]

"How I recite the Hail Mary"

Even today we can read with great pleasure his commentary on each phrase of the Hail Mary. It was found in an undated handwritten document, which we reprint in its entirety here. [Moscati cites the prayer in Latin.]

> To avoid distractions, and to recite the Hail Mary with greater emotion and fervor, I usually refer in my thoughts to an image, or rather, to the significance of an image of the Blessed Virgin, while I recite the different verses of the prayer contained in the Gospel of Saint Luke.
>
> And I pray in this way:

[4] The little statue is now preserved among the souvenirs in the Moscati Room of the Church of the Gesù Nuovo.

Hail Mary, full of grace.... My thoughts hasten to our Lady under the title of Mediatrix of All Graces, as she is represented in the church of Santa Chiara.

The Lord is with thee.... I call to mind the Blessed Virgin under the title of Our Lady of the Rosary of Pompei.

Blessed art thou among women and blessed is the fruit of thy womb, Jesus.... I feel an impulse of tenderness for Mary under the title of Our Lady of Good Counsel, who smiles at me as she is depicted in the church of the Blessed Sacrament Sisters. In front of this image of her and in this church I solemnly renounced impure, earthly affections; *blessed art thou among women*—and if I am in the presence of the tabernacle, I turn to the Most Blessed Sacrament—*blessed is the fruit of thy womb, Jesus.*

Holy Mary, Mother of God.... With my affection I fly to our Lady, recalling the privilege of the Porziuncola of Saint Francis of Assisi. She begged Jesus Christ for the forgiveness of sinners; and Jesus Christ replied that He could refuse her nothing, because she is His Mother!

Pray for us sinners.... I look at our Lady when she appeared at Lourdes, saying that it was necessary to pray for sinners....

Now and at the hour of our death. I think of Mary, who deigns to be venerated under the title of Our Lady of Mount Carmel, protectress of my family; I trust in the Virgin, who under the title of Our Lady of Mount Carmel enriches the dying with spiritual gifts and frees the souls of those who have died in the Lord!

I wonder: is it superstitious to refer to so many images, or rather, to so many titles of the Blessed Virgin during just one prayer? During the Hail Mary?

Moscati's question can only be answered in the negative. It is not superstitious to refer to so many images, because images of our Lord, of our Lady and of the saints are useful and help our devotion. Let us not forget that we are composed of body and soul. His fondness for images was nothing but a sensible development of his deep love.

Moscati was very well acquainted with the Marian liturgical calendar, and he prepared devoutly to celebrate the feasts of our Lady, by fasting also, and every Saturday he abstained from meat. Professor Mazzeo relates:

> Finding himself in a little town of the province of Benevento, where he had traveled to visit a sick priest, he was urged to stay in the house of the local curate, who lived with his brother, a physician. At table, chicken soup was served. The Servant of God asked them not to oblige him to take some, and he was quite willing to eat something else, as long as he could abstain from meat. And so he began to eat bread and olives, which were already on the table. (PSV, §313)

In the collection boxes of the church that he attended there were often considerable offerings for devotions to our Lady and, sometimes, the entire contents of the envelopes that he received for his professional work. Further evidence of this generosity is the fact that after his death these significant offerings were no longer found.

From various testimonies we see how devotion to our Lady was rooted in Moscati's life and work, and how it was part of his spirituality. As for Moscati's favorite titles of the Blessed Virgin, we should recall Our Lady of Pompei and the Immaculate Conception.

Professor Mazzeo informs us that he never missed reciting the *Supplica* [a prayer] to Our Lady of Pompei [at noon, especially on her feast day, May 8], and he recalls a statement by the mother superior of the Sisters of Ivrea, who worked in Vallo della Lucania (Salerno), in the sanatorium of Professor Lettieri:

> Our Servant of God, at the request of Professor Lettieri, traveled from Naples to Vallo della Lucania every first Sunday for consultations in that Sanatorium. On the first Sunday of October in 1920, as he began his consultations, the Servant of God turned to the Superior and said, "Mother, a little before noon, warn me and the others so that we can go to the Oratory to recite the *Supplica*." The mother Superior informed everyone, saying that this was Professor Moscati's wish. Never had such a large number of people been seen in the Oratory! (AM, pp. 315–16)

Moscati traveled to Pompei whenever he could, also to visit his friend Bartolo Longo; he had been acquainted with him since childhood and had become his personal physician. "Tomorrow morning I will come to Valle", he wrote to him one day. "I will go to church and receive Holy Communion, and then I will come to visit you; and I am anxious to tell you that for you I would leave everything, giving you priority over the others."

Bartolo Longo himself had been the one to foster devotion to Our Lady of Pompei among the members of the Moscati family when they, having come to Naples from Ancona, used to attend the Institute founded by Blessed Caterina Volpicelli in the Palazzo Petrone alla Salute.

The lawyer Bartolo Longo had lived there, and he often returned to meet various friends, among them Francesco Moscati and his wife and children. From then on Giuseppe was attracted by the words of that lawyer, who was thirty-nine years older than he and in love with our Lady. From that moment on he attended him for the rest of his life, cared for his health, and visited the nuns, the orphans and the sick whom Bartolo Longo pointed out to him.

In a letter that he wrote to him on September 20, 1926, he said to him:

> From my childhood I have felt drawn to the land where the Queen of the Rosary attracted so many hearts and worked such great miracles. And may she, that kind Mother, protect my soul and my heart in the midst of a thousand dangers among which I sail, in this horrible world!
>
> Whenever I can, I take a trip to Pompei, which many, many times the demands of my profession prevent me from doing nowadays. But whenever I pass fleetingly by train, in view of the Shrine, to travel far for consultations, which happens very often, my glance and my heart are at that place—where through the trees one glimpses the bell tower being constructed—that place beneath the tabernacle over which the image of the Virgin arises!

Moscati visited Bartolo Longo for the last time on the evening of October 3, 1926. Having found that he had double pneumonia, with complications, he exclaimed as he was leaving, "Nothing more can be done! Don Bartolo Longo will leave us in a few days." In fact, death overtook him two days later, on October 5, 1926.

The love of our saint for the Virgin Mary led him to honor her also under the title of the Immaculate Conception. Surely this preference resulted from the purity of his heart and of his sentiments. His chaste life and his flight from every occasion that could disturb his mind put him in tune with the Immaculate Virgin.

One of the churches in Naples that he often visited was precisely the one dedicated to the Immaculate Conception in San Nicola da Tolentino, very near the central funicular railway of the corso Vittorio Emanuele in Naples. In this connection, one very important and eloquent incident is enough to show us his attentive love for our Lady, which caused him to overcome even the sense of physical exhaustion due to long and debilitating travel. This is how Vincentian Father Giuseppe Bottiglieri tells the story in the canonization process.

When asked whether Moscati loved the Virgin Mary, he answered:

> Yes, superlatively, especially in honoring the Blessed Virgin under the title of the Immaculate Conception. I remember that when the fiftieth anniversary of the apparition of Our Lady of Lourdes was being celebrated in the Church of San Nicola da Tolentino,[5] I sent him the program for the devotions. I noted with surprise that during the first three days there had been no sign of Professor Moscati, and only on the evening of the third day was it reported to me that he was in the little grotto chapel. I waited for him at the back of the church, and as he was leaving I of course expressed my surprise

[5] Father Bottiglieri speaks about the fiftieth anniversary of the apparition, but actually it was the fiftieth anniversary of the crowning of Our Lady of Lourdes.

at not having seen him come to the church on that occasion. Professor Moscati replied: "I just returned from the Congress of Medicine in Edinburgh, and at the porter's office I found in my mailbox your invitation and the 'program'. I immediately left my baggage with the porter and ran here to venerate the Blessed Virgin even before seeing my relatives." (PSV, §1417)

Father Bottiglieri relates that in that same church there is a stone (which still exists) with these words that Moscati had engraved on it: "*Veni columba in foraminibus petrae, in caverna maceriae, ostende faciem tuam, monstra te esse Matrem*" [a citation from Scripture, "Come, my dove in the clefts of the rock, in the hollow places of the wall, show me thy face" (Song of Songs 2:13–14, Douay-Rheims), followed by a line from the hymn *Ave maris stella*: "Show thyself a Mother"]. It was his thanksgiving for a lawsuit won against an exorbitant tax levy.

Illumined by prayer, strengthened by the Eucharist, and sustained by love for the Blessed Virgin, Moscati practiced the Christian virtues in a heroic manner and became an example and also a warning to those around him. As we read the testimonies of those who knew him, besides his learning and the human gifts that made him great, we cannot tell what spiritual characteristic to admire the most: his humility, loyalty, understanding for the sufferings of others, detachment from money, kindness, righteousness or charity. Professors, colleagues and students agree in exalting the figure of their student, colleague and teacher respectively.

It is quite true that holiness, authentic sanctity, meets no obstacles in manifesting itself to all!

10

Poor Doctor and Doctor of the Poor

"The sick are the face of Christ"

There are many incidents revealing Moscati's poverty and charity as a doctor toward poor sick people. Indeed, his colleagues and students remember him as the "doctor of the poor".

Before looking at these incidents, we must ask ourselves: How did Moscati ever develop such a great preferential love for the poor?

He himself gives us the answer. On a piece of paper found after his death among the pages of a volume of comparative biology and dated January 17, 1922, he had written: "The sick are the faces of Jesus Christ. Many unfortunate wretches, delinquents and blasphemers come to be admitted to a hospital by an arrangement of the mercy of God, who wants them to be saved! In the hospitals, the mission of the nuns, the doctors and the nurses is to collaborate with this infinite mercy by their help, forgiveness and self-sacrifice."

On another piece of paper, fortunately retrieved by his sister Nina from the wastebasket, Moscati wrote on the evening of June 5, 1922: "Jesus, my Love! Your love makes me sublime; your love sanctifies me, turns me not toward a single creature but toward all creatures, to the infinite beauty of all the beings that are created in your image and likeness!"

When we truly love Christ, we cannot help loving our own brothers and sisters. Moscati was convinced of this, and throughout his life, especially in practicing his profession, he saw the Lord in the sick, to the point of forgetting himself, his own comforts and anything that might concern his own life.

If this is not taken into account, it seems nonsensical to speak about poverty in the life of a man who because of his abilities, genius, fame and social position could have had all the material goods that he desired. Moscati saw Christ in poor sick people, and therefore in order to go meet them he made himself poor.

Everyone who knew him says this, citing particular details of this poverty. Not only was he not attached to money: he gave to the poor what he had. He dressed unassumingly and his sister Nina was the one who looked after his wardrobe. Frugal in his meals, he rejected any sort of affectation.

"He could have become a millionaire if he had wanted," said Professor Michele Landolfi, his colleague and friend, "since he, the 'second Cardarelli',[1] as he was described, held Naples in the palm of his hand; but in the practice of his profession, which became for him a priestly ministry and an apostolate—and that is not just rhetoric—he preferred to practice charity" (GM, p. 132).

Signorina Emma Picchillo, who has already been cited, confirms all this when she says that "by his profession as

---

[1] Cardarelli was a nineteenth-century Neapolitan physician and professor of medicine who worked at the Ospedale degli Incurabili—Trans.

head physician he could have earned great wealth, but he did not value riches, because he lived with his heart detached from them" (PSV, §570).

His colleagues had carriages, horses or automobiles, but he, having none, rode public transportation exclusively or went on foot to visit the sick in the clinics or in the hospitals. Doctor Domenico Galdi, who from 1925–1927 was a medical student in the Lettieri clinic, where he frequently met Professor Moscati, wrote that many directors of clinics (Castellino, Boeri, D'Amato, Bossa, De Carli, Brutti) went to that clinic to treat their own private patients. Moscati, too, went there and, he says, "we young students asked Moscati why he did not have an automobile like his colleagues (indeed, he always came on foot). At that question he became annoyed and said: I am poor; because of my obligations I do not have the means the take on such an expense. I ask you to believe me!" Doctor Galdi then continues: "What he received was destined for the poor, whom he not only treated without charge, but also assisted affectionately, providing their medicine and whatever else was necessary for their livelihood."[2]

Confirming all this, Doctor Enrico Sica testified:

He always had great disdain for temporal things. He loved neither riches nor human glory. His relatives used to urge him to buy for himself a house that was more suitable and more convenient for his profession, but he always resisted them, I think out of love for the virtue of detachment from the comforts of earthly life.

[2] D. Galdi, "Ciò che riceveva era destinato ai poveri", *Il Gesù Nuovo* (1989): 2:92.

For the same reason he never decided to acquire an automobile, even though it would have been immensely useful to him in carrying out his professional work. I wish to note, since I observed it personally, that he, the Servant of God, even while refusing most of his fees, remarkably earned several hundred lire per day on average, and therefore could have led a life of luxury. Yet almost none of that money was spent on his personal conveniences or those of his family. As proof of this I recall an incident in which I personally took part. One day an assistant, Professor Tramontano, during a discussion of the fact that the maestro lived on a third floor, accessible only by an inconvenient staircase, which could prove to be troublesome for some patients, said with a smile, "Professor, with your earnings you could easily install an elevator." To which the maestro replied: "I give you my word of honor that I possess only a bank account with twenty thousand lire." No one can dare to disbelieve Professor Moscati's word of honor. (PSV, §§683–84)

Detachment from money and from worldly goods had become second nature to Professor Moscati, and in his professional work he assigned no importance to his income, much less to creating a life of ease for himself. He kept for himself what was indispensable and the rest he gave to the poor. Obviously his assistants, his students and those who were close to him noticed this disinterest and, profoundly impressed by it, could not fail to testify to it after his death. Therefore there are many significant incidents of his indifference to money and his concern for the poor that we know about.

Professor Gaetano Quagliariello testified that "the money handled by his sister was largely spent on works of charity, with his tacit consent. Even on house calls, if the patients were poor, he took nothing, but instead often left with them a sum of money for the medicines. From ecclesiastics he accepted no compensation; from others he asked for a very moderate fee, to the point of giving it back if he considered it excessive to his way of seeing" (ibid., §1352).

In this connection Professor Mario Mazzeo relates:

> One day a physician friend of mine sent to him for consultation three patients belonging to the same family from Montorsi, in the province of Benevento. At the end of the third visit, the individual who was looking after the patients, unable to tell from the remarks of the Servant of God what fee he demanded, put on his desk a hundred-lire bill and another for fifty. The Servant of God, who usually did not even look at what was put on his desk, was surprised and made a gesture as though of horror; without many words he took the hundred-lire bill and offered it to the person who had given it to him, saying "Fifty lire for all three is already too much; go in peace and say hello to the doctor for me."

Immediately afterward Professor Mazzeo concludes:

> His detachment from earthly things and from the conveniences of life is well known. Practicing the art of medicine as extensively as he did, the Servant of God—had he behaved, with regard to payment, according to the norms established by the health

care profession—no doubt would have been able to amass the financial resources that would have allowed him many comforts. On the contrary, not only did he never mention his rates, which were the minimal fees anyway, but furthermore he either did not accept compensation or else was always content with sums lower than those rates. He did this exclusively out of love for poverty. So too, his love for poverty never allowed him to look for luxurious suits and articles of clothing. (Ibid., §§394–96)

In a deposition for Professor Moscati's process of beatification, Professor Mario Mazzeo was asked how Moscati had behaved in observing the seventh commandment: thou shalt not steal. And his answer was that not only had the then-Servant of God not "profited unjustly in the least by other people's goods" but had always given to others from his own means and from the fruits of his efforts. He then says that he could cite many incidents to prove what he had asserted, but selects from them one told by Doctor Brancaccio from Torre del Greco (Naples) about a low-level clerk from Portici, who had called on Professor Moscati to treat his sick son. Professor Mazzeo relates:

The Servant of God, as he was leaving after the last visit, which was the fourth, agreed to let [the father] offer him an envelope containing the compensation. After saying goodbye and starting down the stairs, he felt an urge (quite contrary to his custom) to take the envelope from his pocket and to see what it contained. Upon noticing the presence of a thousand-lire bill, as though overcome by surprise and disappointment, he quickly went back upstairs, knocked on the door of the flat that he had just left, and when the sick boy's father answered, he said these very words to him, while showing him the envelope: "You have taken me for a madman or a thief", thereby showing his displeasure over the payment that he had received. The poor father, in his initial surprise, got the impression that he was supposed to add more money, and made as though to get more and give it, but the Servant of God, in order to demonstrate with facts rather than with words what he had meant, kept the envelope, but took from his own wallet eight hundred lire and gave them to the sick boy's father, saying that two hundred lire were fair compensation for the visits that he had made. (Ibid., §259)

Professor Mazzeo then adds that although fifty lire per visit were insufficient in the city of Naples, given Professor Moscati's fame, they were even more inadequate if the trip from Naples to Portici is taken into account. Moreover, he states that Moscati, having noted the family's poverty, had taken a modest compensation so as not to humiliate them and at the same time to give the impression that they had paid him.

Another incident, which happened in Torre del Greco, is recounted for us by Father Salvatore Loffredo, a Missionary of the Sacred Heart who had lived in that town from his childhood. One day, he writes, the "doctor from Naples" (as they used to refer to Moscati) was called to the bedside of a sick woman. Moscati first inquired whether she had received the sacraments and then visited her. He found her in a very serious condition, which he did not conceal, and before leaving he accepted the envelope with the fee (one thousand lire), but having noted the family's poverty, said: "I forgot to say something to the patient; may I go back to see her?" He went over to the bed, whispered something, said goodbye to everyone and left. "I do not recall", Father Loffredo relates, "whether the sick woman passed away that same day or during the following night. The family members, helped by good neighbors, started to prepare the body for the viewing by relatives and friends with the bedspreads used at that time. But, to everyone's surprise, beneath the pillow they found the envelope with the thousand lire that had been given to the professor."[3]

The Jesuit Fathers had a preparatory school in Vico Equense (Naples), and they frequently called on Professor Moscati to visit either the religious or the boarding students who were sick. One day Father Antonio Pergola, after the visit, accompanied Moscati to Castellammare, to the "wretched dwelling of a railway man" who had fallen ill. Before anything else the professor advised them to call the pastor, then prescribed a treatment and exhorted those present to have confidence, because the sick man would be cured (as it then happened). Father Pergola says:

> Meanwhile the sick man's coworkers had gathered in one corner of the shabby room to collect the money intended for the professor. And I, who was present, told them that the sum collected by their solidarity

[3] S. Loffredo, "I miei ricordi di san Giuseppe Moscati", *Il Gesù Nuovo* (1998): 3–4/106–7.

with their sick friend would not be accepted by the professor, who offered his services without charge for the benefit of the poor outcasts of society, who were nevertheless dear to his heart, in imitation of Jesus. In fact he, guessing what was happening, asked me what the railway men were doing. I told him that they were collecting money for the fee; then he went over and with eloquent simplicity addressed these few words to them: "Since you, by taking some of your hard-earned money, have come to the aid of your sick friend, I will join in your humanitarian effort and make my contribution to this fund drive, so that the sick man can have, with the sum collected, the necessary means of treating his illness." And he handed over to them three ten-lire bills.

This generous act of the holy man surprised and amazed all present, because they were not used to this unique sort of charity that the professor always practiced; instinctively, without a word, they prostrated themselves at his feet to kiss them as a sign of gratitude and affection. He, though, did not stay for that act of homage but quickly left the hovel.[4]

Countless other incidents are related by those who knew him and were obviously impressed by his consistent conduct, completely detached from worldly goods.

We will not dwell further on it, but, to supplement what has been presented, we report only the testimony of the first honorary president of the Court of Appeals,

[4] E. Marini, *Il professor Giuseppe Moscati della Regia Università di Napoli* (Naples: F. Giannini, 1929), 131.

Alberto Sorrentino, who visited Professor Moscati's house almost every day, having struck up a great friendship with his father, who was also a judge. In speaking about the saint's poverty, he testified that "on the occasion of the feasts of Christmas and Easter, and on his birthday, when he received gifts of food, such as chickens, sweets, and so forth, with his sister's help, he would distribute almost all of them to the poor" (PSV, §§853–55).

And he also informs us of one anecdote that puts Moscati's skill and fame in the same class as Professor Cardarelli's, while at the same time bringing to light his appreciation for the work of his colleagues. Here are his words:

> As a matter of principle, he made his visits to the sick only as an apostolate and not for the money that he might derive from it. He made most of his visits free of charge. I recall now that once in the medical profession there was a set fee for visits to the sick, and both he and Professor Cardarelli received ten lire for house calls to the sick. Because of this small fee and their professional ability, the sick turned to them in droves. The other doctors viewed this as detracting from their own interests, because everyone was consulting the two doctors mentioned above and few went to the others. And so the other doctors decided to ask both Cardarelli and Moscati to increase their fee.
>
> Solely to help his colleagues and not to increase his income, the Servant of God Professor Moscati raised his fee from ten lire to twenty lire, while continuing to make many house calls free of charge. He was completely detached from the goods of this earth. He never made use of the precious gifts that he received. (Ibid.)

These statements by Judge Sorrentino have no need of commentary. Professor Moscati was poor by his free choice and had no fear of appearing to be poor. He had understood that in order to imitate Christ and to give himself totally to his brethren it was not possible to set his heart on earthly goods, particularly money.

Fruitful Chastity

In Church history we find many saintly men who lived a married life with a wife and children, while others preferred celibacy, consecrating themselves to God or living as laymen in the world. Moscati is one of the latter.

Recall the words of Paul VI in his homily at the beatification ceremony: Moscati "is a layman who made his life a mission carried out with evangelical authenticity by marvelously making use of the talents he had received from God" (November 16, 1975).

In his homily at the canonization ceremony, John Paul II said: "This man, whom from now on we invoke as a saint of the Universal Church, appears to us as a concrete fulfillment of the ideal of the Christian layman." He also said: "Truly, every aspect of the life of this lay physician seems to us to be animated by that most typical feature of Christianity: the love that Christ left to his followers as his 'commandment'" (October 25, 1987).

Moscati gave up the chance to start a family and lived chastely, specifically so as to dedicate himself totally to Christ and to his brethren who needed his help. Like other men, he sensed the fascination of beauty and the attraction of the senses, particularly in his youth, but his intense spirituality not only preserved him from the "illusions of love", as he calls them, but also gave his life a direction other than married life that was nevertheless fruitful in works of charity.

Moscati's biographers and many people who knew him agree in declaring that he took a vow of chastity, and they offer as proof what he wrote in his commentary (cited above) on the verses of the Hail Mary. Indeed, after the invocation "Blessed art thou among women and blessed is the fruit of thy womb, Jesus", he says: "I feel an impulse of tenderness for Mary under the title of Our Lady of Good Counsel, who smiles at me as she is depicted in the church of the Blessed Sacrament Sisters. In front of this image of her and in this church I solemnly renounced impure, earthly affections."

If this renunciation of "impure, earthly affections" is the equivalent of a vow of chastity, it is interesting to know that this vow was made, advisedly to be sure, before Our Lady of Good Counsel and in the church of the Blessed Sacrament Sisters, where every day there was and still is exposition of the Most Blessed Sacrament. The Eucharist, our Lady and admiration for the consecrated life give Moscati not only the incentive to offer his chastity to God, but also the strength to preserve it in his professional practice and in every other circumstance.

His work as a physician, his fame and his human qualities certainly exposed him more than anyone else to sensual temptations, but he was always able to keep himself pure and true to his principles. Those around him noticed this virtue of his in his words, his deeds and in all his comportment, and after his death they testified publicly to it.

One student and later assistant of Moscati, Professor Giovanni Ponsiglione, speaking about the virtue of

chastity practiced by the saint, said: "I never noticed in
him any gesture or word that would have offended against
purity, nor did I ever see him read licentious magazines
or newspapers." He went on to tell a story: "I personally observed that when the Servant of God noticed some
woman who was indecently clothed, he would turn his
glance elsewhere. I also recall that one day, in the Hospital,
while visiting a woman who was both hunchbacked and
severely deformed, he said, turning to us doctors who were
around him: 'I prefer a thousand times more this woman
who is in no way responsible for her deformity, and who
is a good person, to some ladies who are beautiful in their
attire and make-up but ugly because of their vices!'" (PSV,
§§1381–82).

Professor Moscati's conduct, while it aroused admiration
and respect for the most part, certainly must have disturbed
those who were not leading an orderly life. Some therefore
raised doubts about the sexual normalcy of the professor or
tried outright to put it to the test with snares.

In his deposition for the beatification process, Doctor
Enrico Sica was explicitly asked "whether the Servant
of God was constrained by some physical defect to be
opposed to marriage". The answer was decidedly negative and deserves to be reprinted in its entirety, especially
because of the wisdom of the argumentation.

> The Servant of God was not impotent. The first proof
> of this is that although he was personally opposed to the
> married state, he encouraged young men to marry if
> he saw that it was necessary for them. This is something
> that those who are sexually impotent usually do not
> do, since ordinarily they harbor a certain envy of those
> who can embrace the married state.

I might add that, when some indiscretion involving women was committed by young men, our Servant of God used to say: "It is necessary to be compassionate with young men because of their exuberance, which not all of them are able to keep in check." I, too, was often present when he made these remarks, because they referred to colleagues whom I knew.

No doubt a spiritually and intellectually mature man like him could not have felt the need to manifest his consideration and compassion for those in the above-mentioned cases, had he not personally and intimately understood the carnal urge.

Finally, the fact that he made a vow of chastity at the age of thirty-four, that is, in the physical and intellectual prime of his life, clearly demonstrates that he knew how to mortify his flesh, while he must have felt all of its urges. He would not have offered to our Lady the renunciation of something that he did not possess. Our Servant of God did not embrace the married state, not in order to be free of the cares of matrimony, but rather for love of the virtue of chastity and so as to dedicate his work completely to God, to science and to his neighbor, as he proved by his conduct at every stage of his life. I have firsthand knowledge of what I have testified. (Ibid., §§635–37)

As we see, there are plenty of reasons to give credence to the testimony of an eyewitness. Professor Moscati had consecrated his chastity to God with full awareness and with the sacrifice involved in renouncing the opportunity to start a family.

One of his biographers, the Jesuit Father Celestino Testore, asserts that "there must have been a moment in the professor's youth when he hesitated between celibacy and the chaste joys of family life. We gather as much from this beautiful page from his diary", which we reprint here in its entirety:

Oh, if only young men in their exuberance knew that the illusions of love are transient, because a lively exaltation of the senses bears little fruit!

And if an angel were to warn those who so easily swear eternal fidelity to illegitimate affections, in the delirium in which they are caught up, that all impure love must die because it is an evil, they would suffer less and be better men.

We become aware of this at a more advanced age, when in the course of human events we draw near, by chance, to the fire that had inflamed us and no longer excites us. I had to examine a woman who, in my first years of my youth, had filled my dreams, and she did not know it. Who would ever have thought that one day she would come to me for consultation?

That beautiful woman was still impressive! And I performed my humanitarian duty calmly, nobly, without a heartstring vibrating within me. She asked me whether I had ever seen her before, so that I might compare her present state with her former excellent health. I answered no. And it was not a lie. The woman from my early years was someone else, who had disappeared without sorrow and without regret, now that my heart was purified![1]

---

[1] C. Testore, *Il professor Giuseppe Moscati della Regia Università di Napoli* (Naples: F. Giannini, 1934), 116.

After reading this page, which is vibrant with humanity but at the same time imbued with higher sentiments, we cannot help pausing in admiration and appreciating Moscati's virtue. His heart, although sensitive like that of all human beings, had been purified of earthly affections and found its peace in God's infinite beauty.

This peace was never disturbed, and more than once it proved to be firm and resolute in overcoming alluring trials. This is confirmed by what happened in Budapest, on a journey that Moscati made together with Professor Quagliariello to participate in the International Congress of Physiology that was being held in Vienna. They both then went to Hungary, and in Budapest Moscati devoted all his time to visiting hospitals and clinics. There a curious incident occurred, which was examined attentively in the beatification process.

Professor Quagliariello testified that in Budapest they were accompanied by a mutual friend, a doctor whom they had met in Naples, who showed them the sights in the city. Then he brought them into a very luxurious house, but as soon as Moscati realized that it was a questionable locale, he decided to leave. In sending to the Promoter General a statement about that incident, Quagliariello confirmed: "Scarcely had Moscati got a sense of those surroundings, when he stood up and said, 'Let's leave!' Which we did immediately."[2]

The episode is eloquent in itself and shows us the moral rectitude of the young professor, who at that time was thirty-one years old. He maintained this attitude throughout his life and kept his heart pure so as to dedicate himself with love to his suffering brethren.

[2] Sacra Congregatio Pro Causis Sanctorum, *Animadversiones de virtutibus*, 47.

His attitude toward the sick, especially if they were women, was always characterized by great propriety, and those who were close to him noticed it and admired it. Some, however, saw him as a rebuke to their own actions, and one day they had a letter delivered to him from a woman who described herself as poor and sick and asked him to make a house call. The saint, moved by the request, went there, but found neither poverty nor sickness: it was a trap. Immediately he went away and did not give the person who had invited him a chance to open her mouth.

Signorina Picchillo, who related the incident and testified to its authenticity, concludes: "Before returning home he went to a church and renewed his consecration to the Lord. Signorina Nina Moscati knew this, partly from her brother himself and partly from a piece of paper from which she gathered that her brother, after overcoming the temptation, had renewed his consecration to the Lord through Our Lady, the Immaculata" (PSV, §567).

Moscati had chosen chastity for himself, but understood very well that this was a gift granted to him by God. He pointed other men toward marriage because, he said, "I consider celibacy the privilege of a few." Therefore he recommended marriage to his students, his assistants and those who came to him for advice. Sometimes he served as their best man.

One of them was Professor Mario Mazzeo, who testified as follows:

> The Servant of God did not contract marriage, not because he was in principle averse to married life or attached to a carefree life without family worries; nor may we think that he was a misogynist. On the

contrary, he frequently recommended marriage to his brothers, his acquaintances and most importantly his students, and I myself am one of those who had the grace of having him as best man. The real reason why he did not marry was his intense love of chastity. (PSV §§166–67)

When we reflect on so many testimonies, knowing that the professor's life was entirely dedicated to others, the question automatically arises: Why did he not become a religious or at least a priest? All the more because he held religious life in the highest esteem and had frequent contacts with priests. It is a legitimate question, and his friends and acquaintances wondered about it, and some did not fear to ask the saint himself.

Professor Guido Piccinino, who knew Moscati from childhood and had been his student and assistant, testified as follows:

> The Servant of God voluntarily chose the lay state. In fact we, his young students, once dared to ask him, in the confidence that he granted us: "Is it true that you, maestro, are thinking of leaving us to consecrate yourself to the Lord in a more perfect state?" He replied: "I think that I can serve the Lord equally well by carrying out the mission of a doctor." (Ibid., §79)

Many other testimonies corroborate these, and they all highlight the professor's anxiousness to serve the Lord in the medical profession. For Moscati, God was not an abstract being, but constantly became concrete, right before his eyes, in the anxieties, sufferings and hopes of the sick. They were not only bodies to heal, but above all souls to save. And he got to their souls precisely through treating their bodies, encouraging others also, especially his colleagues, to act as he did.

Significant in this regard is the recommendation that he made to Doctor Cosimo Zacchino, his former student:

> Remember that you must be concerned not only about the body, but about the groaning souls that turn to you for help. How many pains you will alleviate more easily with counsel, and by appealing to the spirit, rather than with cold prescriptions to be sent to the pharmacist! Rejoice, because your reward will be great; but you will have to set an example for those around you of lifting up your heart to God. (AM, p. 244)

Considering these noble expressions from the heart of Moscati, we understand that for him chastity was not a sterile flight into a solitude devoid of interests and worries, but rather a conscious choice of life for the sake of total dedication to the service of his neighbor. The joy that he recommended to his friend Zacchino, he himself experienced in practicing his profession, to which he had dedicated himself totally, precisely because his heart was free from other affections. Moscati's chastity was fruitful in good works.

While always intent on the good, he was nevertheless able to understand human weaknesses and knew how to joke also. Archbishop Ercolano Marini and Father Celestino Testore reprint a drawing made by Moscati, and the commentary on it by Father Testore himself is very interesting. It helps us to know and appreciate that joyous character trait of the saint, which often flourished in conversation and in his relations with his friends.

His keen wit found a way of showing itself also in an occasional sketch or drawing made by his skillful artist's hand, sometimes in the middle of a conversation, on the first piece of paper or on a simple paper napkin that he found at hand. The one that we have reproduced in this text depicts the field of vision of a modern young lady, with the various blind spots (the housewife's art, cooking, the sanctuary of the home, man's work, the hereafter, true art, study, true virtue) and the "luminous zone" (hairstyles, tailor, heraldry [that is, noble ancestry], fashion, artists, the latest gossip, the art of duping simpletons, or else husbands), is splendid evidence of it and at the same time with its keen wit offers a marvelous lesson that makes you think and reflect seriously.[3]

[3] Testore, *Il professor Giuseppe Moscati*, 137.

12

Lover of Art and Nature

From the testimonies of those who knew Moscati, and also from his writings, a picture emerges of a personality that is mature, both from the moral, religious and professional perspective, and also in terms of intellect and humanity. His gifts fascinated those who were close to him.

This personality could not lack a taste for beauty, which it glimpsed in nature, in art and in the conduct of individuals. Moscati was attracted by flowers, trees, birds, the countryside and everything that human genius has been able to create. Frequently in his writings he makes comparisons, recalls figures and facts from the past and is capable of making visible the natural beauties that surround him or that he manages to discover. There were two occasions in his life on which he expressed himself freely in this regard, manifesting his tastes and preferences: on a voyage to England and France, and on a visit to Syracuse, in Sicily, in November 1925.

Through the letters that he writes, a personality emerges that is unprecedented in some respects: a sensitive man, open to all values and sometimes critical in his judgments. We find an unexpected Moscati also in the observations and judgments that he expresses concerning Naples, the

city that he loved, although he often saw it disfigured by
the Neapolitans themselves.

Journey to England and France

Moscati went to England and France in 1923, four years
before his death, when he was already an established professional. Far from Naples and free from his daily professional duties, he reveals himself in his writing from a new
point of view: he is serene, witty, a fine observer, sometimes critical, as we said, but always ready to admire natural beauties and the masterpieces of the past.

Indeed, in his diary, which he kept from the first days of
the journey, he notes that Paris "is an extremely vast city,
with elegant, densely-populated quarters; it is a sample-
book of various types of cities; whereas Vienna, which I
visited before the war, was quite elegant, well-tended in
the slightest details: in the signboards of the shops with
their all-glass storefronts, in the floral decorations." Edinburgh was more beautiful than London, but he also remarks
that there are "marvelous flowers and fruits in London and
Edinburgh. The house of my hosts", he continues, "is full
of pretty flowers, colossal hydrangeas, delightful gerani-
ums, bluebells; it is full of very beautiful pictures. And then
carpets, fireplaces, etc." (AM, p. 163).

In a letter dated July 26, 1923, he writes: "Here they
go on and on with the flowers: in your room, on the table,
on every nightstand at the hospital, anywhere that you can
put them; you see phaseolus [bean flowers], very beautiful
roses, and so on" (ibid., pp. 170–71). And two days later,
he begins another letter as follows: "It is 7:00: rain. There

is a profound silence, broken only by the chirping of the birds that are abundant here: on the streets, on the windowsills you encounter them" (ibid., pp. 173–74).

Then he depicts London, which he describes as "a boundless metropolis, yet uniform and blackish", while "Westminster Abbey as a house of worship is superb" (ibid., p. 176).

In London, obviously, he visited the museums, and in a letter dated August 1, 1923, he wrote to his relatives:

> The museums of London contain infinite treasures: the British Museum has countless mummies and Greek, Roman and Italian objects. I insisted—against the advice of my companions—on hunting down the famous Rosetta Stone,[1] and I found it there, to the excitement of everyone. The frieze of the Parthenon is there (marvelous!). I wanted to look there also for the bronze objects that were found in our archaeological dig in Mirabella, but no matter how much I toured the place I did not succeed in tracking them down. The National Gallery houses *The Virgin of the Rocks* (Leonardo da Vinci), many paintings by Rubens and Van Dyck: the Flemish and Italian painters are still the joy and the glory of picture galleries throughout the world! One marvelous English painter (or rather American, according to some moderns) is Sargent. Portraits with a suggestive power. (Ibid., pp. 176–77)

Having left England and arrived in Paris, Moscati immediately notes, with his characteristic interest in landscapes

---

[1] This is a stone of black granite which came to light in Rosetta, at the mouth of the Nile, which enabled F. Champollion to decipher the Egyptian hieroglyphs. Moscati was well aware of its importance.

and art, that "Paris is a very beautiful city. It is the city of squares, of stunning buildings, of harmony between monuments, plazas, and esplanades, in the sense that around a jewel of art the French have built a whole suitable scenario. The Opera is delightfully situated, and so are the Louvre and the Tuileries; and the Place de la Concorde has endless views at its various corners of parks, columns, triumphal arches, etc." (ibid., pp. 180–81).

Just as in London he visited the British Museum especially, in Paris he went to the Louvre and thus he writes about it, again to his relatives, on August 5, 1923, following the preceding quotation:

> I saw the marvelous Louvre, filled with incomparable Italian works of art: the most venerable masterpieces, among them the *Mona Lisa* (Leonardo da Vinci); I discovered a *Death of the Virgin* by Caravaggio, which is rather moving, although I could not find a reproduction on a postcard or in any other form. At the Louvre they have the famous Venus di Milo and the Boscoreale Cup (De Prisco); the latter can be viewed only at 2:00 P.M. and it remained unknown to me. (Ibid.)

Here too Moscati proves to be an expert in art and antiquities. The "venerable masterpieces" attract him particularly, and he discovers there the painting by Caravaggio that moves him so much he looks for a reproduction of it, perhaps to keep it and also to send it to his relatives or to his friends. Interesting also is his note about the Boscoreale Cup, which unfortunately he did not manage to see. He certainly was aware that in 1895 in Boscoreale (Naples), on the land of Signor Vincenzo Prisco, by chance a Roman villa had been discovered, in which many vases and other silver objects of Alexandrian and Roman art had been found. He knew also that they were located at the Louvre and now he regrets not having the opportunity to admire them, since he could not reconcile his commitments with the visiting hours.

In France he also visited Versailles, which he describes as "truly marvelous", and then he writes in a letter dated August 4, 1923:

> I saw with great emotion the Galerie des Glaces, where the peace treaty was signed on June 28, 1919. The park is a fairyland come true, with magical wonders and dreams of another age, when people did not yet live on memories and regrets. The palace in the back and the endless avenues that disappear at the horizon; pleasant ponds that reflect green bulwarks of aged trees, tall tunnels of tender green, contained between two ramparts of the dark green of the beeches: it is a delight, and at the same time melancholy. And then the rooms of the palace, besides the Hall of Mirrors, have an impressive richness and unimaginable solemnity. (Ibid., pp. 182–83)

Along with art, Moscati was interested in natural beauties. He notes them immediately and, in describing them, communicates the joy and delight that he experiences. "It is a delight", he writes, "and at the same time melancholy", perhaps because he thinks back to the greenery of his native place, Irpinia, and to all the memories connected with it.

In the diary that he kept in the initial days of that trip, on July 20, 1923, he notes:

We are going through valleys enclosed by mountains that are covered with chestnut trees (Borgone). Here and there the silvery ribbon of the rivers: how similar this scenery is to the unforgettable landscape of Serino, the only place in the world, Irpinia, where I would gladly spend my days, because it holds the dearest, sweetest memories of my childhood and the remains of my dear ones! (Ibid., p. 158)

From Lourdes Moscati wrote only one letter, dated August 6–7, 1923, in which he tells of his impressions and manifests his love for the Blessed Virgin. At the conclusion, he writes that before leaving he ascended by the funicular railway to Pic-du-Jer, from which "one enjoys the marvelous spectacle of the vale of Lourdes and of the snow-covered Great Pyrenees." Then he adds immediately afterward: "There is a fragrance of flowers and herbs there that is just a delight" (ibid., p. 191).

With this expression of love for nature and for flowers he concludes his long epistolary account of his journey. Certainly in the following years—the last three of his life—he recalled what he had seen and admired, regretting perhaps the fact that he could no longer contemplate those "beautiful specimens of the world of vegetation" with which the "Nordic peoples" were supplied.

Journey to Sicily

Moscati certainly was in Sicily in 1922. The journey that is of interest here, however, is the one he made at the end of October and the first days of November in 1925.

He traveled there because he was called to Modica (Ragusa) by Doctor Goffredo Anello, who wanted him to visit a friend of his who had heart disease. On the trip back he stopped in Syracuse, and from there he wrote two letters to his doctor-friend in Modica. The second, dated November 2, is rather long and interesting.

"After our farewell, at the station in Modica," he writes, "on the train I immersed myself in reading the signs of Sicilian civilization" (ibid., p. 252).

This sentence is noteworthy, because it allows us to see his interest in art and also his eagerness to admire the Sicilian civilization, which, as he goes on to say immediately afterward, was a dream that he had as a child and that now was becoming a reality. Let us read his account, which is expressive and full of feeling.

> This morning I attended the Masses commemorating the deceased in an impressive convent chapel. And then, with the weather overcast, I went to breathe the atmosphere of classical antiquities, which have always been my passion. I saw the Greek theater, the amphitheater, the stone quarries. What emotion I experienced at the phenomenon of the echo and resonance, at the Ear of Dionysius [a carved limestone cave]! When I was a boy I used to read in physics treatises about this phenomenon in Syracuse; I was moved by the account of the torments of the prisoners, whose trembling words were conveyed to one's ear by the powerful resonance of the place; I became fascinated by the legends and myths of the land of Syracuse that were celebrated by Ovid.... At a distance of so many years, the things that had been the subject of my dreams and aspirations to learn more and more about classical

culture became a thrilling reality for me that morning. And all the fond pleasures of my earliest age would have sought to trouble me with the memory thereof, and to compel me to repeat with the Catanese poet Felice Romani: "but those days I find no more!", had I not already armored my heart and soul against the seductions of lost goods and adopted the motto: Do not look back, but yearn instead for the future and for future perfection!

I see that, without knowing it, I am boring you with my sentimentality, which often crops up.

But allow me for just a moment to turn to a sentimental theme, hoping to return, not as a physician, but as a friend and a tourist to the Sicilian coasts, confronted by the blue of the sea and blue of the sky, and populated by ruins of ancient civilizations, all of them the symbol of the divine imprint of the kiss received by man from God, and extraordinarily rich in generous hearts. And among those cities I would never omit Modica. (AM, pp. 253–54)

This excerpt from a letter presents to us a Moscati who is little known and unexpected. It is a discovery that catches us unprepared, yet arouses our interest and admiration. If we have visited Syracuse, we certainly have had the same sentiments and the same emotions that he now manages to express in a few deft strokes. The phrase, "I went to breathe the atmosphere of classical antiquities, which have always been my passion", shows us not just a simple love for ancient art, but something that goes down deep, to the innermost roots of his soul, and now becomes "a thrilling reality", cloaked with sentiment and "aspirations to learn more and more about classical culture".

Interesting too, in the excerpt quoted, is the citation from Felice Romani, the author of poems, literary criticism and opera librettos. Among other things, he is the librettist of *La Norma* and *La sonnambula* by Vincenzo Bellini and of *L'Elisir d'Amore* by Donizetti. Here Moscati, a lover of music and operas, quotes from memory a verse from *La sonnambula*: *"Ma quei dì non trovo più."*

Upon returning to Naples, Moscati kept corresponding with his friend and colleague, to whom he wrote four letters. In one, written on January 30, 1926, he tells him: "I have very pleasant memories of my stay in *'la bella Sicilia'*. Although I missed the enchantment of the blue, I had instead the warmth and friendship of you and of all who welcomed me" (ibid., p. 256). It must have cost Moscati a lot not to have been able to see Syracuse with "the enchantment of the blue" skies and sea for which it is famous, since, as he had written before, he had gone to "breathe the atmosphere of classical antiquities" "with the weather overcast". But now, recalling that day, he thinks again of the warmth and friendship that he found and considers himself fortunate.

Love Naples but denounce its evils

From the age of four Moscati had lived in Naples, where he moved with his family in 1884. He loved the city "like his native land", he wrote in one letter. "It has its flaws, but in our city there is a tendency to make efforts to compete with the north" (ibid., p. 117).

Moscati noted and denounced these flaws, especially in 1919, after the end of the [First] World War, when there was talk about a local strategic plan for Naples. He was experiencing its urban problems and, foreseeing what might happen next, he wrote to the Municipal Council a long letter that is not well known but of great current interest. In it he also manifests a fine aesthetic sense.

Here we reprint only a few passages. He begins by referring back to the eruption of Vesuvius and the earthquake of Messina and says that then there were "alarming Cassandras" who had whispered a similar calamitous omen for Naples, although he had remained incredulous. "But now I have changed my opinion", he continues.

> No earthquake, no Vesuvius, no cataclysm will ever destroy Naples ... but the Neapolitans may. The little of its enchanting slopes and hills that has remained intact will disappear shortly due to the merchants' rage for building. And so much that is historical, and the most beautiful villas and palaces are threatened by the pick ax of the urban planners; the *aediles* [Roman officials in charge of public works], if we may call them that, who are supposed to protect the aesthetics of the city and the countryside, are like sleeping dogs who let thieves steal.
>
> The moment is propitious: there is a lack of housing, it is necessary to build. Anything is justified: erecting skyscrapers, raising them high on the hilltops; demolishing the old parks so as to cram barracks there.... And beautiful Naples is dying; suffocated by the ruins of houses. (Ibid., p. 358)

Moscati foresees the havoc that will take place (unfortunately he was a true prophet!), and with poetic nostalgia he thinks back to the beauties of Vomero, Posillipo and several villas—architectural marvels that are disappearing.

In Naples, redolent of its April orange groves and melodious with birds, there will no longer be room for grass. What will be left of the infinite gradations of color on the hills of Vomero and Posillipo, changing with the sun, in the first breeze of spring, covered with almond trees in bloom? The long green brush strokes of the slopes, suspended between the celestial hue of the sea and the celestial hue of the sky, will be the substratum of a mosaic of stones.

The summit of the Vomero district, overwhelmed by geometric tenement houses, by now has a Cubist profile, similar to the zig-zag braid on an Italian major general's cap. The pines and cypresses of the Villa Patrizi, overshadowing the classical panorama of Naples along with Mount Vesuvius found in all the photographs and picture postcards, may be awaiting their end with fear and trembling.

The dark evergreens of the Villa Salve, once freely exposed to the wind, tower in order to stretch out over the huge, emaciated tenements that crown the heights of the via Tasso. And the Villa Clorinda, on the promontory of Sant'Antonio, which is covered by a patchwork of dark foliage with a thousand vent-holes open to the sky, like blue disks, and then heated red hot at sunset, seems to fall headlong, undermined by excavations for new buildings. And how many rapacious eyes are on the garden of the piazza Amedeo: it is a prisoner sentenced to death, over whom the surrounding buildings stand guard. (Ibid., pp. 358–60)

Then, turning to the mania for new construction, he writes:

> The collective delirium that there is a need for housing causes the citizenry to resign itself to all the damage. And shortly even the blessed solitude of the Camaldolese will be violated, and right beneath the Hermitage the calm rustling of the oaks and chestnuts will be replaced by the rumbling of the elevator and by coffee house music and cinemas. Farewell to the poetry of the solitary "little house painted pink"!
>
> No more trellises of the rural inns, with their hummingbird vines, spangled by the scarlet of the blood-red flowers, and with their grape clusters continually surrounded by the humming of bees, like a submissive song to productive nature. They will be replaced by penthouses with their art nouveau windows! (Ibid., p. 361)

These remarks may present to us an unexpected Moscati, different from the way in which he is ordinarily portrayed; but it is he. His clear sight and serene mind do not allow the beauty of nature to be defiled, nor do they tolerate human selfishness gaining the upper hand. Obviously, human beings also have to live and build a roof over their heads in the midst of these beauties, but their demands must be moderated so as to find a balance that reconciles personal needs, taste and harmony. He writes:

> Housing is necessary, yes, and it is also preferable that Naples grow rich on villas at the enchanting spots, provided that they are delightful, instead of on tenement blocks, inasmuch as these villas will serve exclusively to

let the *nouveaux riches* themselves who spend the winter
in the city enjoy the panorama. But a sense of propor-
tion is necessary, and above all an aesthetic sense. Let
us throw open the doors and the balconies to the sun
and to the sea breeze; let us build verandas so that they
break up, with their wisteria and their damask draperies
of bougainvillea and of ampelopsis reddening in the
autumn, the monotonous line of windows, symmetri-
cal as wide-open eyes. (Ibid., p. 362)

Finally, Moscati points out another problem that is fundamental for Naples but unfortunately was never solved.
He himself suffered from this lack of a solution, since he
was forced to travel frequently in making house calls to his
patients. Therefore he recommends a transportation project by the city planners and envisages tunnels and new
roads "while respecting the old city of Naples".

The conclusion of his letter is emotional and at the same
time realistic:

But if they continue to crowd building projects into
Naples, which is already densely settled, farewell to the
beauty of the panorama. And the emigrant who returns
to Naples thirty years from now, no longer impressed
by the divine spectacle of the green, flowering Neapolitan landscape, situated on the sea, no longer differenti-
ating hills but seeing only a huge amphitheater-shaped
tenement block with a thousand windows, will fearfully
repeat the words of the prophecy: "Here Naples once
was." (Ibid., p. 363)

13

Sudden, Silent Death

The story goes that one day someone asked Saint Aloysius Gonzaga, then a Jesuit student, while he was playing a game, what he would do if he knew that he would die in a short time. The saint replied: "I would continue to play."

If this question had been posed to Professor Moscati in the early afternoon on April 12, 1927, we certainly would have had a similar answer. Since he was seeing patients during office hours at his home, he would have continued his work. When one is at peace with God and is doing one's duty, one is always ready to commend one's soul to God.

Precisely on April 12, 1927, Holy Tuesday, Professor Moscati had attended Mass and received Communion, as he did every day; he had spent the morning at the Ospedale degli Incurabili, teaching and visiting the patients on Ward III, and had returned to his home, on the via Cisterna dell'Olio, together with his student Giuseppe Tesauro. He had a frugal meal and then his usual consultations with the patients who came to see him. Among them was Signora Teresa Carulli-De Marsico, who upon entering had noticed a sign of weariness on her doctor's face and had pointed it out to him: "Professor, how are you?"

"When you're working, you're well", had been his answer.

When the visit was over, the woman had said good-bye to him and gone down the stairs with her daughters Teresa and Eugenia. Immediately afterward—it was three o'clock—the professor felt ill, leaned back in an easy chair, crossed his arms and peacefully breathed his last. He was forty-six years and eight months old.

The sad news spread immediately and the sorrow was universal: men of science, colleagues and students, priests and religious communities, but above all the poor people, were all dismayed.

"How sorrowful this hour is for us, O Professor Moscati," said Professor Giovanni Castronuovo, "for we have thus unexpectedly lost the light of your counsel, the peace of your consolation, the fullness of your almost prophetic aspirations, and the example of your inexhaustible charity!" (GM, p. 57). And the Cardinal of Naples, Alessio Ascalesi, after praying in the presence of the body, turned to the family members and said: "The professor did not belong to you but to the Church. When he went up he was greeted not by those whose bodies he healed, but by those whose souls he saved."[1]

The funeral ceremonies, which were held two days later, on Holy Thursday, were a triumph, and the newspapers of the day published long, detailed accounts.

We reprint here only what was written in the April 15–16 issue of *Il Mattino* under the headline: "The Grief of All Naples around the Coffin of Giuseppe Moscati".

[1] E. Marini, *Il professor Giuseppe Moscati della Regia Università di Napoli* (Naples: F. Giannini, 1929), 353.

Around the mortal remains of Giuseppe Moscati were reverently assembled all the citizens, with each class represented, from the humblest to the most elite. On few occasions has Naples witnessed a spectacle so impressive in its boundless sorrow, which goes to show how much affection, esteem and admiration had been won by the man who was able to turn his profession into a very noble apostolate, who was able, with the beneficial aid of his teaching, to lavish his unparalleled goodness on all who were suffering, and who was able to demonstrate how, marvelously, religion and science can be reconciled in a noble mind.

All of the notable figures in our city, starting with His Excellency [Antonio] Casertano, the President of the Chamber of Deputies, the senators, the deputies, the municipal authorities, the scientists, physicians, surgeons, university professors, judges, the representatives of the Forum, the most elite aristocracy, the students and an immense crowd of friends, admirers and disciples, followed the remains of Giuseppe Moscati. It is absolutely impossible to catalogue that immense multitude, because if we tried to set about such a task, apart from the enormous space that would be required, we would necessarily fall into a great deal of omissions.

At ten o'clock, the whole via Cisterna dell'Olio was literally packed. The coffin, borne on the shoulders of Professors Ninni, Tramontano, Tesauro, Briganti, De Maio, Ponsiglione and Rescigno, was set down on the hearse. (GM, pp. 35–36)

In the guest book placed at the entrance to his house was found, among others, a very significant anonymous inscription: "You did not want flowers, or tears either: but we mourn the fact that the world has lost a saint, Naples has lost an example of all the virtues and the poor sick people have lost everything!"

Recalling these moving words, Professor Gaetano Quagliariello wrote:

> No, unknown devoted brother, the world did not lose a saint, because saints are not lost. They live in eternity, and their charitable and apostolic work does not end with their brief life on earth: they are the guide, the perennial example to this humanity which so often, too often, loses the way of its truth, of its sole destiny: being reunited in eternity with God the creator of all things. (PSV, §1072)

14

A Saint Sixty Years after His Death

Giuseppe was raised quickly to the honors of the altar: he was a saint sixty years after his death and one hundred seven years after his birth. The esteem and the veneration that had surrounded him during his lifetime literally exploded after his death, and soon the sorrow and the mourning of those who had known him were turned into emotion, enthusiasm and prayer. In the presence of his coffin, surrounded by civil authorities, leading figures and especially by the poor people whom he had helped, many expressed their sorrow and praised the virtues of the deceased; the newspapers (*Il Mattino*, *Roma*, *Il Giorno* and others) published extensive reports of the funeral; those who had been close to him felt his absence and sorely missed him.

In the writings and testimonies of everyone, however, readers immediately began to find portents of something that went beyond a simple remembrance, something that was turning into admiration of sanctity. Professor Giuseppe Tesauro put it very well when he said:

> The affection and devotion that I had for him during his lifetime were changing into a different feeling,

something profound and serene that I cannot quite define. Something like devotion to a saint, to a higher being. I still sense his vigilant intellect: I find in that intellect all the consolation that I need; I also feel that I am helped and guided by it! And in saying this I am not exaggerating in the least. Today sorrow no longer is part of the feeling that binds me to his memory: it is a strong, calm religious bond, to which I feel more attached every day.

Every time I went to the Pilgrims' Chapel at Camposanto—where he is buried—even on the days when there was no pilgrimage, there was always someone kneeling there (at his tomb); most often completely unknown persons who were poor![1]

His confessor asked the relatives of the deceased, two days after his death, to keep the clothing and the objects that had belonged to him, because they were now transformed into relics, and God would make use of them for his greater glory.

The fact that everyone kept not only his letters but also his prescriptions is also worth reflecting on. Never was it known, not even in the cases of the most famous physicians, that so many private persons jealously kept and then handed down to their descendants the prescriptions written by their doctors. Thanks to this jealous concern, hundreds of prescriptions penned by Saint Giuseppe Moscati are preserved in the archives. Even now from time to time we receive photocopies of the saint's writings and sometimes even the original documents.

[1] C. Testore, *Il professor Giuseppe Moscati della Regia Università di Napoli* (Naples: F. Giannini, 1934), 159–60.

Little by little, as time passed, the memory of the professor did not wane at all but rather grew, and his tomb, in the Pilgrims' Chapel of Poggioreale Cemetery (Naples) was the destination of continual pilgrimages. The family members received letters from all over, the commemorations followed one after the other, and newspapers throughout Italy published reports. The biography written by the Archbishop of Amalfi, Ercolano Marini, in 1929 was soon sold out, and the following year a new edition was published. Concerning this book, Father Agostino Gemelli wrote: "His biographer, for all the material with which he has filled these pages, still leaves the reader guessing that there is something more, and gives the distinct impression of a wealth that still remains not entirely revealed to the astonished eyes of his contemporaries."[2]

On November 16, 1930, at the request of various representatives of the clergy and the laity, the Archbishop of Naples, Cardinal Alessio Ascalesi, permitted the transfer of the body from the cemetery to the Church of the Gesù Nuovo. On that day the spectacle of three years earlier was repeated. Not only the contemporary press coverage but also the photos that have been preserved clearly show the extent of this manifestation of faith and of love for the "saint of Naples", as everyone by then referred to Giuseppe Moscati. The body was entombed, in the presence of Cardinal Ascalesi and the bishop of Campania, on the right side of the chapel of Saint Francis Xavier, where a stone (which still exists) indicated the spot for the devotion of the faithful who were coming ceaselessly in great numbers to pray and beg for graces.

[2] A. Gemelli, "Una esemplare figura di medico cristiano", *Vitae Pensiero* (1930): 226.

Meanwhile, on July 6, 1931, at the Archbishop's Chancery in Naples, they began the informative process. That was the first official act along the path toward canonization.

At that time, besides Moscati's brothers Gennaro and Eugenio, his sister Anna was still living; she was known by everyone as "Nina" and had a fundamental role in Giuseppe's life and sanctity. Speaking about the works of charity performed by the saint, his brother Eugenio said: "As his accomplice in doing good he had our sister Nina."

That she was "complicit" with her saintly brother is the greatest thing that can be said in praise of this woman, who for years, silently, humbly and intelligently, was able to stand by a man who was famous yet led a special life that was different from that of his colleagues who were seeking fame, honors and riches. She was the one who took care of her brother and not only looked after his personal needs but also assisted him in his works of charity and spiritual aid. She often visited the families pointed out to her by her brother, bringing material aid and offering Christian consolation.

Nina Moscati was highly meritorious, not only for the works of mercy and the apostolate to which she had consecrated her life, but also after her brother's death for having helped preserve what belonged to him. Guided by the Jesuit Father Giovanni Aromatisi, she donated to the Church of the Gesù Nuovo her brother's clothing, his household goods and furniture, including his bed and the easy chair on which he had expired. Moreover, together with Father Aromatisi and, as was mentioned, at the request of leading figures, she obtained permission to transfer the body from Poggioreale Cemetery (Naples) to the Church of the Gesù Nuovo.

As fame of his sanctity spread and was confirmed, many people flocked to the Church of the Gesù Nuovo to pray at Moscati's tomb. Meanwhile the Tribunal for the Causes of the Saints proceeded to examine his writings, and to gather testimonies about his life and his practice of the virtues and about the prodigies worked by the Lord through his intercession.

The *Decree on the heroic virtues of the Servant of God Giuseppe Moscati*, issued by the Congregation for the Causes of Saints on May 10, 1973, outlines the course of that process:

> The reputation for holiness that the Servant of God enjoyed during his lifetime grew even more after his death, so much so that after scarcely four years had passed, the diocesan investigations were initiated at the Neapolitan Chancery in 1931, and then, once the commission to introduce the cause was established on March 6, 1949, the process concerning his virtues was scheduled for the years 1950–1952. All the testimonies agree in asserting that, in his state and condition of life, the Servant of God ceaselessly practiced these virtues, both theological and cardinal and the others associated with them, in a way superior to other Christians and which is styled heroic; this was happily approved by a unanimous vote both at the special meeting of the bishop- and priest-consultors on November 7, and also in the Plenary Congregation of the Cardinals on December 19 of that same year.[3]

In the meantime, since two miracles had been attributed to the intercession of Professor Moscati, one from

[3] *Acta Apostolicae Sedis* 65 (1973): 460–61.

January 26, 1956, to August 19, 1957, in the Diocesan Chancery of Pozzuoli, the other from May 9 to October 9, 1951, in the Diocesan Chancery of Calvi and Teano, the processes were prepared. Subsequently the documents were forwarded to the Congregation for the Causes of Saints. On September 18, 1974, the Medical Commission, appointed by that same Congregation, declared those cures scientifically inexplicable; then, on June 17, 1975, the Cardinals unanimously decided in favor of their supernatural character. On October 3, 1975, the *Decree of Authenticity of the Miracles* was promulgated in the presence of Paul VI.

On November 16, 1975, Paul VI declared Giuseppe Moscati Blessed during the celebration of Mass in Saint Peter's Square.

In 1977, the fiftieth anniversary of the death of the Blessed, plans were made to improve the accommodations for his earthly remains. On August 29 the Congregation for the Causes of Saints authorized Cardinal Corrado Ursi, Archbishop of Naples, to proceed to a canonical recognition of the body, which was carried out affectionately and lovingly by Professors Felice D'Onofrio, Giuseppe Tesauro and Giuseppe D'Ambrosio. On November 16 the remains were reposed beneath the altar in the Visitation Chapel, in an artistic bronze urn, the work of the sculptor Professor Amedeo Garufi.

Meanwhile devotion to the Blessed increased more and more; the faithful frequently had recourse to his intercession and numerous favors were attributed to his intervention. Selected from among these was the cure from acute myeloblastic leukemia of the young man Giuseppe Montefusco that took place in 1979.

The acts of the process, conducted at the Regional [Ecclesiastical] Tribunal of Campano di Napoli, were sent to the Congregation for the Causes of Saints. The Medical Commission, on December 3, 1986, unanimously confirmed the lethal diagnosis of acute, nonlymphoid leukemia and "the relatively rapid modality of Montefusco's complete and lasting cure, which cannot be explained according to scientific knowledge".

On March 27, 1987, the Congress of theologians, based on the favorable opinion of the Medical Commission on the preternatural character of the aforesaid cure, "agreed in acknowledging the adequacy and validity of the juridical and theological evidence" and in recognizing the connection—as a *strict cause-and-effect relationship*—between the invocations addressed to Blessed Giuseppe Moscati (and exclusively to him) and the prodigious event of the healing.[4]

After this favorable opinion, expressed by the cardinals of the Congregation for the Causes of Saints on April 28, 1987, John Paul II, in the consistory on June 22, 1987, set the date for the canonization as October 25 of that same year.

In that period, as was mentioned, from October 1–30, in Rome the Seventh General Assembly of the Synod of Bishops was being held on the topic of "The Vocation and Mission of the Lay Faithful in the Church and in the World" twenty years after the Second Vatican Council.

November 16: liturgical feast of Saint Giuseppe Moscati

For Christians, death is birth into heaven, and therefore the feasts of the saints are celebrated on the day of their departure from this world. The feast of Saint Giuseppe Moscati ought to be celebrated on April 12 of each year, since he

---

[4] *Congressus super miro* (March 27, 1987), 41–42.

died on that day. The Archbishop of Naples, however, asked the Congregation for Divine Worship to transfer the feast to November 16 because of "pastoral reasons" and received a positive response.

These reasons can be summed up as follows: the first two weeks of April always coincide either with Holy Week or with the celebration of the Resurrection of our Lord. Therefore it would never be possible to celebrate the feast on April 12.

They might have chosen October 25, the day of his canonization, but they preferred November 16, because on that day in 1975 Giuseppe Moscati was beatified by Paul VI and also because on that same day, in 1930, the mortal remains of the saint were transferred to the Church of the Gesù Nuovo and reposed on the right side of the altar of Saint Francis Xavier, where the stone marker is still preserved.

In 1977, as was mentioned, they were placed beneath the Altar of the Visitation, in an urn sculpted by Professor Amedeo Garufi. The urn is composed of a triptych, which sums up the professional work of the saintly doctor: university professor, consoler inspired by the Eucharist, hospital physician.

At all hours of the day, in front of this urn, the faithful pause in prayer, and frequently, before leaving, they kiss and grasp the hand of the saint sculpted on the central panel. They make the same gesture with the hand of the bronze statue placed on the left side of the altar (as the viewer faces it), the work of the Venetian sculptor Pier Luigi Sopelsa. Both hands are shiny because of the continual contact that the thousands of persons who visit the tomb want to have with the saintly doctor. The statue is two point four meters [almost eight feet] tall and was blessed by Pope John Paul II during his pastoral visit to Benevento, the birthplace of the saint, on July 2, 1990. Shortly thereafter it was transported to Naples. With this work Professor Sopelsa intended to pay homage to the saintly physician in return for an extraordinary grace received by his wife, Signora Armida.

15

Three Miracles for the Beatification and the Canonization

After the death of Professor Moscati, many healings of various sorts were attributed to him, and these ceaselessly continue to occur even now. God, the sole author of a miracle, can meet the needs of human beings in prodigious ways through the intercession of the saints.

The Church, which accomplishes the work of Christ on earth, is very cautious in making declarations about miraculous events and examines them carefully for the purpose of beatifying and canonizing one of her members who during his lifetime heroically put the Christian ideal into practice. According to the legislation in force until 1983, for Moscati's beatification two miracles were required, whereas the new norms provide that only one is enough for this stage.

The three miracles attributed to the intercession of Professor Moscati and approved by the Congregation for the Causes of Saints took place respectively in 1954, 1941 and 1979.

First miracle

This was the healing of senior prison warden Costantino Nazzaro, who was born in Avellino on May 22, 1902, and lived in perfect health until 1923, when he had a cold abscess at the root of his right thigh and pains in his spinal column. After being admitted to the Military Hospital in Genoa and then dismissed, without having obtained any positive outcome, during his convalescence he experienced numbness and enlargement of the right epididymis, of tubercular origin, treated by the application of X rays and by a surgical intervention. Despite these treatments, Nazzaro was not cured; not only that, but he still had a fistula. Furthermore the disease spread to his left side.

In 1929 he married, and with fairly good health continued to work as a prison warden, first in Avellino, then in Rome.

His physical condition began to worsen in 1943, and two years later, in 1945, he was visited by Doctor Giuseppe Dante di Pozzuoli who had been a student of Moscati. Here is his testimony:

> When I examined Nazzaro for the first time, in early 1945, that is, when he, as a prison warden, first reported sick to me, since I was the medic at the institution, I noted the following: remarkable deterioration; profound asthenia and anemia; patches of hyperpigmentation on the exposed parts, face, hands and neck; irritability; premature male climacteric; cyclic vomiting; stubborn constipation alternating with profuse diarrhea; hypotension; fast pulse rate. I therefore made the diagnosis of Addison's disease and prescribed a hormone-based therapy.[1]

[1] Sacra Congregatio pro Causis Sanctorum, *Neapolitana: Beatificationis et canonizationis Ven. Servi Dei Iosephi Moscati ... Positio super miraculis: Miracolo primo* (Romè, 1975), 61.

The diagnosis was confirmed by other physicians who examined and treated him. In the meantime, indeed, Nazzaro had been transferred from Rome to Pozzuoli (Naples) and had been examined also by Professor Giovanni Di Guglielmo, head of the medical clinic of the University of Naples.

In all textbooks of medical pathology, Addison's disease was described as a very rare condition, always with an unfavorable prognosis; a fatal outcome was certain. Because cases of healing were unknown, therapy served merely to prolong the patient's resistance. Despite the treatments, in fact, Nazzaro did not improve and, as his wife recalled, "the doctors gave him no hope and their prognosis was always negative."

In the spring of 1954 the sick man, after entering the Church of the Gesù Nuovo and seeing many believers praying before the tomb of the Servant of God Professor Giuseppe Moscati, began to pray for his own healing, and for about four months he returned there every two weeks. In his family, too, prayers were sent up to the Servant of God, and the Holy Rosary was recited every day before an image of him.

The patient's wife, Signora Luigina Francalanci, in her testimony, confirmed everything, stressing that, once human remedies failed, they turned to the Servant of God Giuseppe Moscati, who had been a physician.

Summer had arrived, and one night, between the end of August and the beginning of September of 1954, Nazzaro dreamed of being operated on by Professor Moscati, who replaced the atrophied part of his body with living tissues and told him to stop taking any medicine. When he woke up, he found that he was completely healed and soon returned to his job, from which he had been on leave for quite some time. As might be imagined, his coworkers and friends wanted to celebrate his return with a festive dinner at a restaurant in Pozzuoli. The health care professionals who examined the former patient could not explain the unexpected healing.

In 1957 Costantino Nazzaro, on behalf of the ecclesiastical authorities, was examined carefully and at length by two physicians, Doctor Giuseppe Di Gennaro and Doctor Salvatore Perito, who found him in the best of health. They testified that his complexion had become brown and uniform again, and the pigmented spots on his lips and gums that were characteristic of Addison's disease had disappeared. His pulse was strong and regular.

The man who had been miraculously cured died on February 7, 1963, from heart failure.

Second miracle

Raffaele Perrotta was instantaneously cured of meningococcal cerebrospinal meningitis, in the night between February 7 and 8, 1941.

As is plain from the dates, Costantino Nazzaro was cured more than thirteen years after Raffaele Perrotta, but the Congregation for the Causes of Saints examined Nazzaro's cure first, which therefore is listed as the first miracle.

Born in Calvi Risorta (Caserta) in 1928, little Raffaele, a first-year secondary school student at the Convitto San Tommaso D'Aquino in Piedimonte d'Alife, experienced vertigo, vomiting and pains at the base of his neck on February 2, 1941, during the celebration of Mass in the chapel of the boarding school. Doctor Giuseppe D'Amore, who was called in to make a diagnosis, suspected meningitis and ordered that the patient be isolated and sent back to his parents' house in Petrulo, a neighborhood of Calvi Risorta. Doctors Marrocco and Di Benedetto confirmed their colleague's diagnosis: meningoencephalitis with petechial manifestations on the abdomen.

In order to make sure, Professor Pirera from the University of Naples was consulted. After examining the patient, he confirmed the diagnosis and suggested a lumbar puncture [spinal tap]. This confirmed the serious meningeal process.

Meanwhile the patient's condition had worsened: high fever, tremor, pupillary rigidity with anisocoria [pupils of different sizes], conjunctivitus, agitation and delirium. His parents had already prepared the white garment for his burial.

In the meantime the pastor in Petrulo, Father Giovanni Zumbolo, realizing the gravity of the case, brought to the patient the image of Professor Giuseppe Moscati in a white gown.

"Seeing that human remedies had failed," the patient's mother, Signora Carmela said in her testimony, "Giuseppe Moscati was invoked. His image was placed under the pillow. In church, too, prayers were offered; I prayed with all my soul. No promise was made, only to publish the miracle if one was granted. And afterward that is what we did."[2]

The mother goes on to relate what happened then:

A few hours after Professor Pirera left, the boy was conscious: he recognized everyone. During the night

[2] Ibid., *Miracolo secondo*, 15.

he slept; the next morning his condition was improved, so much that the doctors, Di Benedetto and Marrocco, said that he had no need of treatment. They did a spinal tap and said that there was no longer any disease in the fluid. On that same day the boy started to eat, because until then he had not kept anything down. He quickly and completely regained his strength. He was eating pasta, soup, everything.

In testimony dated May 10, 1951, Doctors Marrocco and Di Benedetto confirmed what had happened, asserting that two things were indisputable: the gravity of the illness that caused them to foresee the boy's death and the immediate healing.

Raffaele Perrotta continued his studies and devoted himself to teaching until his retirement. He married in 1955 and had six children. He is still grateful to the saintly physician, his benefactor, and with his whole family he participated in the beatification ceremony on November 16, 1975. In 2004 he was still living in his birthplace, Calvi Risorta, in the province of Caserta and enjoyed very good health.

Third miracle

Present at Moscati's canonization, which took place on October 25, 1987, in Saint Peter's Square, was twenty-nine-year-old Giuseppe Montefusco, the third recipient of a miracle, who presented to the Pope a wrought-iron face of Christ that he himself had made. Indeed, he is by trade an ironworker in Somma Vesuviana (Naples), where he was born on May 15, 1958.

This tall, well-built young man, who now is in excellent health, in early 1978, at the age of twenty, began to complain of weakness, pallor, vertigo and lack of appetite. Since his red blood cell count and platelets were extremely low, on April 13, 1978, he was admitted to Cardarelli Hospital in Naples, by order of his physician, Doctor Luigi Di Palma.

At the hospital all the health care professionals agreed on the diagnosis: acute myeloblastic leukemia: a serious form of neoplasm of the granuloblastic stem which, in the days before chemotherapy and cytostatic drugs, led in the more or less short term to death. It is evident from the medical literature that only a small percentage of patients suffering from acute, non-lymphatic forms of leukemia survive more than five years, even if high-dose chemotherapy treatment is given in intense cycles.

Doctors Renato Di Girolamo, Carlo De Rosa and Renato Montuori administered support therapies and blood transfusions to the patient in various cycles until June 1979, that is, for a little more than a year; then Montefusco no longer allowed his condition to be monitored and did not repeat the maintenance cycles. He had also resumed his heavy labor as an ironworker and was leading a normal life. What had happened?

His mother, Signora Rosaria Rumieri, still tells everyone quite simply and emphatically what occurred. Discouraged by the negative diagnosis given to her son, one night in a dream she saw the photograph of a physician in a white gown, to whom many people were bringing offerings. She too joined them and offered two thousand lire. In the morning she told the pastor all about it, and since he told her that the doctor was surely Professor Moscati, whose body was found in the church of the Gesù Nuovo, she went there. She was startled to see the picture that she had dreamed. She asked whether she could get a copy, and when she asked how much it cost, she heard the reply: an offering of two thousand lire!

It is easy to imagine what happened next in the Montefusco household: relatives and friends prayed ceaselessly before the image of Professor Moscati, sending up their petitions to God and reciting the Rosary. Montefusco's father, Signor Antonio, affirmed that every day they prayed before the picture of the Blessed, frequently applied his image to the young man's chest, and often went to the church of the Gesù Nuovo. Giuseppe too, while in the hospital, continually prayed to the Blessed, whose image was placed on a ledge beside the bed. Meanwhile he suddenly began to improve, and after less than a month he was perfectly cured.

In a medical report dated February 4, 1986, Professor Angelo Tirelli and Doctor Armando Marano declare that in his present status Signor Montefusco appeared clinically and hematologically healthy. Professor Renato Montuori, the head of the Nineteenth Hematology Division of Cardarelli Hospital, who at the time of Montefusco's initial recovery was an aide in that same Division, was also able to confirm that same clinical status. He declared that on November 7, 1985, he had reexamined Giuseppe Montefusco after around six years and had observed the persistent remission of the disease, after performing peripheral blood tests and taking samples of the marrow and of the cerebrospinal fluid.

Doctor Luigi Palma, Montefusco's family physician, who in April 1978 had ordered Giuseppe's admission to the hospital, related the whole incident in a deposition for the Causes of Saints, and concluded that Montefusco, despite his very stressful job as an ironworker, was well and from 1979 on had no other significant illness.

A medical panel appointed to examine the case evaluated the clinical documentation, then unanimously decided that the healing of Signor Giuseppe Montefusco was extraordinary, and sent to the theological consultors and then to the cardinals a report that expressed their positive opinion, declaring that it was possible to speak of an inexplicable healing.

On January 22, 1987, Jesuit Father Paolo Molinari, postulator of the cause of canonization, asked the Pope to proclaim Blessed Giuseppe Moscati a saint, emphasizing that "the forthcoming Synod dedicated to the role of the laity in the Church could have in the canonization of Blessed Moscati a realistic illustration of what the Church expects of those who live out their baptism according to their specific duties."

The request was granted and the physician from Naples was canonized on October 25, 1987, in Saint Peter's Square. As of this writing [2004], Signor Montefusco is more than forty-five years old and from time to time pays a visit to the saintly doctor. Every year without fail he celebrates his feast day.

He married in 1988, and during the concelebrated Mass on November 16 his young wife presented her bridal bouquet at the altar; then in 1989 the couple appeared with their little daughter who had been born shortly before, to whom they gave the name Giusy [nickname for Josephine] in memory of Giuseppe Moscati and so as to celebrate her name day precisely on November 16 each year.

The mother of the man miraculously cured still keeps the picture of Professor Moscati that she bought for two thousand lire, and still shows everyone her joy and gratitude to the one who cured her son.

APPENDICES

RELEVANCE OF THE MESSAGE
OF SAINT GIUSEPPE MOSCATI

As an appendix to this presentation of the life and personality of Saint Giuseppe Moscati, it is essential to reprint some remarks and thoughts taken from his writings. Many of them have already been quoted in the preceding pages; here we repeat some and add others: they are a message that is still relevant for everyone.

As we have seen, Moscati was filled with God, always acted in his presence and when speaking or writing communicated his convictions with vibrant, captivating expressions. The fact that so many friends and acquaintances preserved his writings—the ones that we have now—is clear proof that Moscati's thoughts and expressions touched souls and did not leave people indifferent.

To read them and reflect on them at various times and in different situations of life can give us courage, hope, light and serenity. For us, too, they can be incentives to reflect and—why not?—an aid in our personal prayer.

If we are willing to listen to him, the saint can speak to our hearts, can communicate his spiritual wealth and exhort us to love God and our neighbors.

The following texts are reprinted in chronological order.

1. *As a boy Moscati looked at the windows of the Hospital of the Incurables and was moved by the thought of the suffering people who were there. He wrote this to Senator Giuseppe D'Andrea*

after being appointed director of the Third Men's Ward at that same hospital (July 26, 1919).

> As a boy, I looked with interest at the Ospedale degli Incurabili, which my father pointed out to me in the distance from the terrace of our house, inspiring in me feelings of pity for the nameless suffering that was alleviated within those walls. A salutary dismay seized me, and I began to think of the transitory character of all things, and my illusions passed away, as the flowers fell from the orange groves that surrounded me. Then, being thoroughly occupied by my initial literary studies, I did not suspect and did not dream that, one day, in that white building, at whose windows could scarcely be distinguished, like white phantoms, the hospital patients, I would one day hold a position at the top of the clinical hierarchy.... I will endeavor, with God's help, and with my insignificant powers, to live up to the trust that is placed in me, and to collaborate in the economic rebuilding of the old Neapolitan hospitals, which are so worthy on account of their charity and culture, but so poor today. (AM, pp. 110–11)

2. *Everything in life passes and then a better world opens up, where we will be reunited with our dear ones in the Supreme Love. From a letter to a lawyer by the name of Mariconda, who had lost his sister* (February 27, 1919).

> Life is an instant; honors, triumphs, riches and knowledge fail, before the fulfillment of the cry of Genesis, the cry flung by God against guilty man: "You shall die!" But life does not end with death, it continues

in a better world. To everyone has been promised, after the redemption of the world, the day that will reunite us with our dear departed ones, and that will bring us back to the supreme Love! (AM, p. 274)

3. *Signorina Carlotta Petravella had lost her mother. Moscati reminded her that life is a flash of lightning in comparison with eternity and that it is a daughter's duty to pray for and to be united with the deceased through Holy Communion* (June 20, 1920).

I tell you with conviction that your mother did not leave you and your sisters: she is watching over her children invisibly, now that she has experienced, in a better world, the mercy of God and is praying and asking for consolation and resignation for those who mourn her on earth.

I too, as a boy, lost my father, and then, as an adult, my mother. And my father and mother are beside me; I sense their pleasant company; and if I seek to imitate them, who were just, I have their encouragement, and if I do something wrong, I have their good inspirations, as once during their lifetime I had their spoken counsels.

I understand your anguish and that of your sisters; it is the first true sorrow, and the first time that our dreams are shattered; it is the first call of your thoughts as a young woman to the realities of the world. But life has been described as a flash of lightning in eternity. That is our humanity. Because of the merit of the suffering that permeates it. The suffering that satiated the One who was clothed in our flesh and transcends matter and leads us to hope for happiness beyond this world.

Blessed are those who follow this lead of the conscience and look "to the hereafter", where the earthly
affections that seem to be prematurely broken off will
be restored.... I remind you of one of your duties as
a daughter: honor the memory of your dear departed
mother, not only with your words and the praise that
wells up from a soul trained to see what is beautiful, but
also in a more profoundly human manner, inasmuch
as it satisfies the sentiments, in a way that will be the
balm and comfort of your heart: with prayer to God,
with Communion with God, sublime union, that it
might count for the one that in her final moments your
mother would not have disdained. (AM, p. 276)

4. *A nephew of Doctor Roberto Silvestro had liver cancer and
cirrhosis of the liver. Moscati writes to him and reminds him that
when there is nothing more that human beings can do, it is necessary to take refuge in God* (September 17, 1920).

What can men do? What can resist the eternal laws of
life? There you have the need to take refuge in God.
But in any case we physicians must seek to alleviate the
sufferings. (AM, p. 278)

5. *Being unable to attend Doctor Giuseppe Biondi's party cele-
brating his doctorate, Moscati reminds him that he has assumed
responsibility for a sublime mission* (September 4, 1921).

But know that, with the same affection with which I
accompanied you from your third year of coursework,
I am with you in spirit, in the midst of your friends,
who are applauding you, alongside your parents and

relatives, who have tears of tenderness and pride, because you have gained the reward of your intelligence and tenacious will.

Remember that in pursuing medicine you have assumed responsibility for a sublime mission. Persevere, with God in your heart, with the teachings of your father and your mother always in your memory, with love and devotion for the abandoned, with faith and enthusiasm, deaf to praises and criticisms, steadfast against envy, and inclined only to do good. (AM, pp. 231–32)

6. *Doctor Cosimo Zacchino, from Lecce, anxious about personal problems, writes to Moscati, who had been his teacher. He receives from him a reply exhorting him to have confidence: God abandons no one* (October 6, 1921).

Whatever may happen, remember two things:

God abandons no one.

The more alone, neglected, despised and misunderstood you feel, and the closer you feel to being overwhelmed by the weight of a grave injustice, you will have the sense of an infinite, mysterious power that sustains you and makes you capable of good, manly purposes, the force of which will astonish you when you become calm again. And this power is God!

You must remember something else, namely that there is no need to be disheartened, but rather you should put into practice one of the four cardinal virtues, fortitude. To become disheartened means to vindicate the motives that others allege in order to impose on us one way of thinking rather than another. (AM, p. 242)

7. *In 1922 Moscati had attained great scientific maturity and renown, but he was beginning to notice visual disturbances that might limit his activity. After his death a piece of paper with the following handwritten notes, dated January 17, 1922, was found in a book.*

The sick are the faces of Jesus Christ. Many unfortunate wretches, delinquents and blasphemers come to be admitted to a hospital by an arrangement of the mercy of God, who wants them to be saved!

In the hospitals, the mission of the nuns, the doctors and the nurses is to collaborate with this infinite mercy by their help, forgiveness and self-sacrifice.

By harboring grudges in our hearts, we end up neglecting this mission, entrusted by Providence to those who aid the sick; the sick are also neglected. Every now and then, however, the Lord gives a sign of his presence and awareness. Suddenly a sick person dies, who was not able to attract and surround himself with loving care! We hope that the Lord may be close to him, at the final moment! (AM, p. 56)

8. *Moscati's prayer to Jesus, who was his love. Found by his sister in the wastebasket.*

Evening, June 5, 1922.

Jesus, my Love! Your love makes me sublime; your love sanctifies me, turns me not toward a single creature but toward all creatures, to the infinite beauty of all the beings that are created in your image and likeness! (AM, p. 56)

9. *Not science, but charity has transformed the world. . . . These words of Moscati are found in a letter written to Doctor Antonio Guerricchio, from Matera, his former assistant. There are sublime expressions throughout the letter.*

Naples, July 22, 1922.

My dear Guerricchio, I have meditated a great deal on your precious letter. I felt undeserving of your gratitude and your praises. But above all I have my past; and how many young men I have remembered who were promising, full of the spirit of sacrifice and of virtue, imbued with a true enthusiasm, yet ended up missing in action, overwhelmed by the nepotism, indifference and egotism of the priests of science!

But certainly it will not be that way with you: because even though you are obliged to be far away, in surroundings that are at least purer, in a less stifling atmosphere than that of the City [Naples], you will nevertheless be able to nourish the insatiable thirst for knowledge and to organize your work in a manner more in keeping with the human conscience, in other words, with the good of your neighbor, with the charitable ideal.

Not science but charity has transformed the world, in some eras; and only very few men have gone down in history because of their science; but all men can remain imperishable, a symbol of eternal life, in which death is only a stage, a metamorphosis for the sake of a higher ascent, if they dedicate themselves to doing good.

In my heart there is still a keen regret, knowing that you are far away; the only thing that consoles me is that you have preserved within yourself something of me; not because it is worth anything, but because of that spiritual message that I strove to uphold and spread around: a sublime task, but so unattainable with my meager strength.

I keep you in mind, be sure of it.... I kiss you, in Christ! Very affectionately yours, Giuseppe Moscati. (AM, pp. 248–49)

10. *Doctor Agostino Consoli had regularly visited Moscati's ward at the Hospital of the Incurables and, after completing his course of specialization, wrote to the maestro to thank him.*

In reply he received a short letter dated July 22, 1922, which is a program of life. In it we find the famous phrase: "Only one science is unshakable and unshaken...."

Although you are now far away, do not stop cultivating and reviewing your medical knowledge every day. Progress is found in a continual critique of what we have learned. Only one science is unshakable and unshaken, the one revealed by God, the science of the hereafter!

In all your works, look to Heaven, and to the eternity of life and of the soul, and then you will have a very different orientation from the one that merely human considerations would suggest to you, and your work will be inspired for the better. (AM, pp. 370–71)

11. *"Love the truth": this is the program of life that Moscati proposes for himself after meeting with various sorts of opposition. Three days after passing his qualifying examination to teach clinical medicine, he wrote these words on a piece of notepaper dated October 17, 1922, which his sister Nina found in the wastebasket.*

Love the truth, appear as you are, and without affectation and without fear and without human respect. Even if the truth costs you persecution, accept it; and if it means anguish, endure it. And if for the sake of truth you should have to sacrifice yourself and your life, then be strong in your sacrifice. (AM, p. 57)

12. *"Remember that life is mission; it is duty; it is suffering!" This is the encouragement that Moscati gives to Doctor Cosimo Zacchino, who participated in a competition for municipal doctor.*

Naples, Ascension Thursday, 1923.

My dear Zacchino, do not be sad! Remember that life is mission; it is duty; it is suffering! Every one of us must have his battle station. If God wills that you practice your noble profession among the people in the countryside, it means that he wants to make use of you to sow good in those hearts.

Remember that you must be concerned not only about the body, but about the groaning souls that turn to you for help. How many pains you will alleviate more easily with counsel, and by appealing to the spirit, rather than with cold prescriptions to be sent to the pharmacist! Rejoice, because your reward will be great; but you will have to set an example for those around you of lifting up your heart to God.

Grottammare is a very beautiful place to live: I am acquainted with it. Take advantage of the Easter season to draw near to God in Holy Communion, and take from Him inspirations for your future career.

I kiss and embrace you. Gius. Moscati. (AM, p. 244)

13. *The first medicine, infinite love: so Moscati wrote to one of his patients, Signor Tufalli from Norcara, who was returning to Calabria, to his home sweet home and his mountains* (June 23, 1923).

> There is only one glory, one hope, one greatness: the one that God promises to His faithful servants. I ask you to remember the days of your childhood and the sentiments handed down to you by your dear ones, by your mother; go back to practicing your faith and I swear to you that, besides your spirit, your body will be nourished thereby: you will heal in both soul and body, because you will have taken the first medicine, infinite love. (AM, p. 339)

14. *"God ... floods souls with ever greater resignation." In Lourdes Moscati participated in the procession of the sick and describes it with emotion to his relatives* (August 6–7, 1923).

> A handsome paralyzed boy stands with his little hands joined and his darling eyes turned toward the white Host; the blind, uncertain, turn their extinguished eyes toward the place where they hear but do not see the eternal light; a long series of thin, emaciated, moaning women, skeletal as mummies, clasp their rosary beads. And the Host passes by silently. No healing! God, who in an instant can restore life, who is omnipotent, turns to their hearts, to their souls, and floods them with ever greater resignation.
>
> Did not Bernadette, the one to whom the Blessed Virgin first appeared, remain an asthmatic, and was she not a paralytic in a chair for the last eight months of

her life? When the round of the sick is completed, the procession resumes, and from the steps of the Rosary Basilica the priest raises the monstrance to the three corners of the world and gives the benediction. (AM, p. 191)

15. *It is an obligation in conscience to instruct the young men, without concealing from them one's own experience. Moscati writes to Professor Francesco Pentimalli, who invited him to be a member of the commission that was supposed to organize the hospital assistants* (September 11, 1923).

I thought that all the meritorious young men who have set out on the path of medicine, amidst the hopes, the sacrifices and the anxieties of their families, should have the right to perfect their skills by reading a book that was not printed in black and white but rather has as its cover the hospital beds and the laboratory rooms, and as its contents the suffering flesh of human beings and scientific material—a book that must be read with infinite love and great sacrifice for one's neighbor.

I thought that it was an obligation in conscience to instruct the young men, shunning the current fashion of jealously keeping secret the fruit of one's own experience, but rather revealing it to them, so that, scattered later throughout Italy, they might truly bring relief to the suffering for the glory of our University and of our Country. (AM, p. 116)

16. *Everything passes; only love remains eternally. Moscati consoles a friend from Lecce, the notary De Magistris, whose daughter had died.*

Naples, March 7, 1924

Dear Sir, I have here on my desk, among the first flowers of spring, the portrait of your daughter, and I pause, while I write, to meditate on the transitory nature of human things!

Beauty and every charm of this life passes....

The only thing that remains eternal is love, the cause of every good work, which outlives us, which is our hope and our religion, because God is love. Satan sought to defile earthly love too, but God purified it through death. Majestic death which is not the end but the beginning of the sublime and the divine, compared to which these flowers and beauty are nothing!

May your little angel, snatched away in the freshness of her youth, like her beloved friend, whom she met again in recent days, Blessed Thérèse,[1] help you and her mother from heaven and may she pray and care for you and protect and thank you.

---

[1] Moscati was very devoted to then-Blessed Thérèse of the Child Jesus. He speaks about her in several letters and had a picture of her in his room. In the diary that he kept during his journey to England, he noted on July 18, 1923: "God had warded off from me the occasions of sin, and for several months now He has been giving me, in His infinite kindness, a very pleasant calm, and a few days ago I was reading in the autobiography of Blessed Thérèse of the Child Jesus a sentence made for me: 'Discouragement too, my God, is a sin.' Yes, it is a sin of pride, because it makes me think that it is possible to have accepted an opinion of oneself as though one had done great things! Whereas one has always been a useless servant." Even then Moscati realized what John Paul II wrote in the Apostolic Letter *Divini amoris scientia* (October 19, 1997), on the occasion of the proclamation of the saint a Doctor of the Church: "To everyone Thérèse gives her personal confirmation that the Christian mystery, whose witness and apostle she became by making herself in prayer 'the apostle of the apostles', as she boldly calls herself, must be taken literally, with the greatest possible realism, because it has a value for every time and place."

Yours truly, with the most sincere gratitude. Gius. Moscati. (AM, pp. 284–85)

17. *Moscati reminds Doctor Antonio Nastri, from Amalfi (Salerno), about the privileged position of a doctor, who often finds himself in the presence of souls who are anxious to find some consolation* (March 8, 1925).

The physician is then in a privileged position, because he often finds himself in the presence of souls who, despite their past errors, are on the verge of surrendering and returning to the principles that they inherited from their ancestors, and stop there, anxious to find some consolation, tormented by their pain. Blessed the doctor who can understand the mystery of these hearts and inflame them once again.

But there is no doubt that true perfection can exist only by detaching oneself from the things of the world, by serving God with a constant love, and by serving the souls of our own brethren with prayer, with our example for a great purpose, for the one purpose that is their salvation. (AM, pp. 325–26)

18. *The physician, in a patient's final moment, must remember that he has before him not just a body but also a soul, a creature of God, Moscati writes to his colleague Giuseppe Borgia in October 1925, after examining a friend of the latter and confirming his fatal diagnosis.*

Alas, if our science were completely cold and destined solely to maintain the petty pleasures of the body, what use would it be? It would be a handmaid of materialism and egotism!

And therefore to protect it from such an accusation, we physicians, in a patient's final moment, such as the one our friend is in, must remember that we have before us not just a body but also a soul, a creature of God. And I hope that our patient has made provisions for that great step and that his better half has urged him to do so.

I assure you that through my continuous studies and my acquaintance with the various peoples of Europe and with their customs, I have an ever more deeply rooted belief in the hereafter: the human genius, which is so powerful, capable of manifestations of beauty and truth and goodness, can only be godly; and the soul and human thought must return to God. (AM, p. 68)

19. *In 1925 the Jesuit Father Giuseppe De Giovanni and Professor Mario Mazzeo published a little book entitled* Eugenics. *Moscati wrote the preface in which, among other things, he recommends continence to young people . . . as a practice of self-denial and sacrifice.*

All young people should understand that the practice of continence is the best way to keep away from the worst contagious disease, which is the symbol of original sin, syphilis, and, by keeping their spirit and their heart far from depravity through the practice of self-denial and sacrifice, ought to swear to give their adulthood and their sexual health solely to the one whom they love exclusively. (AM, p. 353)

20. *Doctor Francesco Pansini, having fallen ill, was visited by his teacher Moscati, who afterward sent him this letter, reassuring him but reminding him to work for the greater glory of the Lord.*

Naples, January 30, 1926.

My dear Pansini, you know that I have been caught up in a whirlwind of inescapable duties. That is why I did not write to you sooner! I want to kindle your hope once again, to turn it into certainty: you will recover! God then will demand of you an accounting for the life that He will give you.

And a thousand years from now, when you appear in His presence, you must be able to answer: "Lord, I spent the day well! I worked for Your greater glory!"

So, you will recover; but be patient, it takes time. Do not forget to feed your soul by the reception of Our Lord in Holy Communion, just as you feed your body—and that is your unavoidable duty.

Cordial greetings. Affectionately yours, Gius. Moscati. (AM, p. 228)

21. *While Doctor Francesco Pansini was convalescing, the thesis that he had submitted in order to be promoted to assistant instructor in physiology was read. Moscati wrote to him that evening, Wednesday, March 10, and gave him the news of his promotion, praised him and told him that someone who does not abandon God will always have a sure and upright guide in life.*

My dear Pansini, this evening we read your thesis. It was an enormous success. A marvelous thesis, the best that we have judged thus far.... Everyone on the board could only applaud. I heard whispering: "That's a lot of physiology." "Yes," I proclaimed, "that's a lot of clinical experience—modern clinical experience based not on empiricism or the stereotypical questions and answers of semiology, but on physio-pathology and modern methods."

I don't need to tell you that I had to bite many bullets! The ones belonging to many of the contestants who were approved and promoted! But what can be done about it? However, for my part I lured the other colleagues. I assure you that even the competitors present in the auditorium had to bow to your thesis and acknowledge its superiority.

I received the excerpts from your work and thank you. But it made me especially glad to hear that you are on the way to recovery. Let us allow God to do His work! And you will see that someone who does not abandon God will always have a sure and upright guide in life. Setbacks, temptations, and passions will not prevail to sway someone who has taken, as his ideal, work and knowledge [wisdom], of which the *initium est timor Domini* [Latin: fear of the Lord is the beginning]. (AM, p. 229)

22. *Moscati frequently visited and also wrote to his friend Bartolo Longo. On July 20, 1926, in a letter, he confided to him that from his childhood he had felt drawn toward the region where the Queen of the Rosary attracted so many hearts.*

From my childhood I have felt drawn to the land where the Queen of the Rosary attracted so many hearts and worked such great miracles. And may she, that kind Mother, protect my soul and my heart in the midst of a thousand dangers among which I sail, in this horrible world!

Whenever I can, I take a trip to Pompei, which many, many times the demands of my profession

prevent me from doing nowadays. But whenever I pass
fleetingly by train, in view of the Shrine, to travel far
for consultations, which happens very often, my glance
and my heart are at that place—where through the
trees one glimpses the bell tower being constructed—
beneath the tabernacle over which the image of the
Virgin arises! (AM, pp. 315–16)

23. *"The few pennies that I have, I have to leave to beggars like
me." So Moscati wrote to one of his nephews by the name of
Franco, the son of his brother Eugenio.*

Naples, evening of February 1, 1927.

My dear Franco, do you think that I am your rich
uncle in America? I am poor: that is the whole story.
And no one loves the poor. But it is good that I tell
you this, because if on the one hand you stop courting
me, on the other hand you will talk no more nonsense!

The few pennies that I have, I have to leave to
beggars like me. If I were to leave them to you, you
would squander them on various stupid things. You
should work, work, work. Learn well your lessons at
school, learn the modern languages. Spend the time
that you waste on movies and idleness in improving
your education. In that way you will gain treasures
which in the future will yield glory and wealth for you.

But always be humble, even when you have won
praise and applause. I am sending you five hundred lire,
which cause me concern, and how! And reflect that
you could do so much good but are not doing it: you
could be a good example to your family and friends,
be an angel of kindness, patience, studiousness; be an

example of religious perfection. Read good books, the examples of so many youths who by meekness, sacrifice, and prayer to God drew non-practicing relatives to God (mind you, I am not talking about your relatives). But if you keep on being a "good boy", then ... that is a different kettle of fish.

Regards. Peppino Moscati. (AM, p. 226)

24. *The laws of divine wisdom govern not only the colossal objects in the cosmos but also the very delicate fabric of the most microscopic element. These are Moscati's thoughts, expressed in a discussion with Professor Pietro Castellino and then reported by the latter after the death of the saint.*[2]

Nothing prevents us from accepting the idea that matter is animated by a great number of profound energies that develop it in its workings and in the progressive complexity of its forms, but it is necessary likewise to maintain that this principle of spirituality which aspires to develop itself and to manifest its efficacy gradually, that this marvelous order which is organized within matter until it reaches the highest summits of its most elaborate organization, is none other than the proof that a *Deus absconditus* [hidden God] rules with supreme intelligence this superb edifice upon which life arises, which occurs thanks to laws sanctioned by the Most-High Wisdom that moves everything; these laws are all the more marvelous inasmuch as they govern not only

[2] A. Marranzini, "Giuseppe Moscati un esponente della Scuola medica napoletana", *Orizzonte medico* (Rome, 1980): 174–75.

the colossal objects in the cosmos but also the very delicate fabric of the most microscopic element.

25. In one of his diaries, Moscati wrote the following words, which ought to make young men especially reflect. They are the fruit of his self-denial and also of his sacrifices.

Oh, if only young men in their exuberance knew that the illusions of love are transient, because a lively exaltation of the senses bears little fruit!

And if an angel were to warn those who so easily swear eternal fidelity to illegitimate affections, in the delirium in which they are caught up, that all impure love must die because it is an evil, they would suffer less and be better men.

We become aware of this at a more advanced age, when in the course of human events we draw near, by chance, to the fire that had inflamed us and no longer excites us. (AM, pp. 347–48)

26. On an undated piece of paper addressed to Signora Enrichetta Sansone, a former patient of his (he had later served as the best man at her wedding to Angelo Zuccardi), Moscati writes these sentences, which are helpful to everyone in every age.

Value life! Do not waste time in recriminations about lost happiness, in fretting. *Servite Domino in laetitia.* [Serve the Lord with gladness.]

An accounting for every minute will be demanded of you! "How did you spend it?" And you will answer, "Weeping. [*Plorando.*]" You will hear the retort: "You ought to have spent it by praying [*implorando*], with your good works, and by overcoming yourself and the demon melancholy."

And so! Get up and get to work! (AM, p. 366)

27. *The memorable words that follow were pronounced by Moscati on the occasion of the dedication of a bust of Giovanni Paladino in Poggioreale Cemetery.*

The need to immortalize great departed figures in marble and bronze, and to celebrate their work, goes to show that human thought and the human soul are eternal.

Beneath every cross and every pillar in this cemetery, where it seems that the graves enclose nothing but piles of shapeless bone and dust, there is the memory of a heart that lived on infinite love and suffered an immense pain; this is the resting place of a soul that cannot be extinguished. The work of so many great men commemorated here defies the centuries, symbol of the divine imprint on those brains from which it sprang.[3]

28. *Signorina Emma Picchillo declared in her deposition: I remember that [Moscati], while speaking with me about the love of God, said:*

Let us love the Lord without measure, which is to say, without measure in sorrow and without measure in love…. Let us place all our affection, not only in the things that God wills, but in the will of God Himself who determines them. (PSV, §501)

---

[3] A. Marranzini, *Giuseppe Moscati il laico santo di oggi* (Rome: AVE, 1978), 261.

29. *"It is true, it is true that the Lord's yoke is easy and light. When we love the Lord, sufferings are no longer felt, and if they are, they become sweet. As we come to love the Lord intensely, we desire and love repentance." Moscati spoke these words one day to Signorina Emma Picchillo, in Pompei, after hearing her sing: "The yoke of the Lord is easy and light." The same young woman testified that in a letter he wrote to her:*

> Let us practice charity every day. God is love: he who abides in love abides in God and God in him. Let us not forget, every day, and even every moment, to make an offering of our actions to God, doing everything for love of Him. (PSV, §495)

30. *In a fragment found by the Jesuit Father Alfredo Marranzini among Moscati's papers, these words are written, which certainly guided him in his visits to the sick:*

> Suffering should be treated not as a twitch or a muscular contraction, but as the cry of a soul, to whom another brother, the doctor, runs with the ardent love of charity. (AM, p. 63)

PRAYERS

For physical and spiritual health

O Saint Giuseppe Moscati, renowned doctor and scientist, as you practiced your profession you treated the body and the soul of your patients; protect us also who now confidently turn to you.

Give us physical and spiritual health, by interceding for us with our Lord.

Relieve the pain of those who suffer, give comfort to the sick, consolation to the afflicted, hope to the discouraged.

May young people find in you a model, workers—an example, the elderly—a comfort, the dying—hope for an eternal reward.

Be for us all a sure guide in the practice of diligence, honesty and charity, so that we might perform our duties in a Christian manner and give glory to God our Father. Amen.

For a sick person

O holy doctor Giuseppe Moscati, who, enlightened by God in the practice of your profession, gave to so many

These prayers are taken from the volume *Preghiere in onore di san Giuseppe Moscati*, edited by Antonio Tripodoro, S.J. The text in Italian can be ordered from: Padri Gesuiti, Chiesa del Gesù Nuovo, via San Sebastiano, 48, 80134 Naples, Italy. website: www.moscati.it; e-mail: moscati@gesuiti.it people health in body along with health in spirit, grant that N., who at this moment needs your intercession, may recover physical health and peace of mind.

May N. return soon to work and, together with you, thank God and praise him in holiness of life, always mindful of blessings received. Amen.

For a dear person

Saint Giuseppe Moscati, who during your life showed concern for the persons who were dear to you, and devoted yourself to them by helping them, counseling them and praying for them, I ask you, protect N., who is especially dear to me. Be his guide and comfort and direct him toward the path of goodness, so that he may act uprightly, overcome every difficulty and live serenely in joy and peace. Amen.

Prayer of young people

O Saint Giuseppe Moscati, you had a special love for young people. You defended them and wrote that it is "an obligation in conscience to instruct the young, shunning the current fashion of jealously keeping secret the fruit of one's own experience, but rather revealing it to them."

I pray you to help me and to give me strength in the struggles of life. Enlighten me in my work, direct me in my choices, support me in my decisions. Grant that I may live these years as a gift from God, received so that I may help my brothers and sisters. Amen.

For deceased relatives and friends

O Saint Giuseppe Moscati, who because of your merits have received the reward of eternal life, intercede with God so that my deceased relatives may enjoy eternal rest. If because of their frailty they have not yet attained the beatific vision, be their advocate and present my petitions to God.

Together with you, may my dear relatives and friends protect me and my family and guide us in the decisions and choices that we make. By living a holy, Christian life, may we one day be able to rejoin them so as to praise God, our joy, together with them. Amen.

ABBREVIATIONS OF SOURCES

AM   Alfredo Marranzini. *Giuseppe Moscati modello del laico cristiano di oggi.* Rome: AVE, 1989.

GM   Gennaro Moscato (brother of the saint). *Giuseppe Moscati* [a collection of remembrances and newspaper reports, tributes, speeches, telegrams, etc., on the occasion of his death]. Naples: F. Giannini, 1927.

GQ   Gaetano Quagliariello. "Giuseppe Moscati". *Medicus* 4 (1948): 86–100.

PSV   Sacra Congregatio Pro Causis Sanctorum. *Neapolitana: Beatificationis et canonizationis servi Dei Iosephi Moscati viri laici: positio super virtutibus.* Rome: Guerra e Belli, 1972.

BIBLIOGRAPHY

Bergamini, Paola. *Laico cioè cristiano: San Giuseppe Moscati medico*. Genoa: Marietti, 2003.

D'Onofrio, Felice. *Giuseppe Moscati: Medico, docente, santo*. Naples, 1995.

Marranzini, Alfredo. *Giuseppe Moscati, il laico santo di oggi: Scritti inediti*. Rome: AVE, 1978.

———. *Giuseppe Moscati: Modello del laico cristiano oggi*. Vol. 1. Rome: Edizioni ADP, 2003.

———. *Giuseppe Moscati: Un esponente della scuola medica napoletana*. Vol. 2. Rome: Edizioni ADP, 2004.

———. *Nina Moscati, sorella del medico santo*. Rome: Edizioni ADP, 2004.

Papàsogli, Giorgio. *Giuseppe Moscati: Il medico santo*. 3rd ed. Milan: Paoline, 1998.

Tripodoro, Antonio. *Giuseppe Moscati: Il medico santo di Napoli visto attraverso i suoi scritti e le testimonianze dei contemporanei*. 2nd ed. Naples, 1999.

———. *Preghiere in onore di san Giuseppe Moscati*. 3rd ed. Naples: Chiesa del Gesù Nuovo, 1994.

Tripodoro, Antonio and Egidio Ridolfo. *San Giuseppe Moscati e il Gesù Nuovo*. Naples, 2000.

INDEX OF PERSONAL NAMES